GARDENING WITH
TULIPS

GARDENING WITH
TULIPS

WORDS AND PHOTOGRAPHS BY **MICHAEL KING**

TIMBER PRESS

Gardening with Tulips
Copyright © Frances Lincoln Limited 2005
Text copyright © Michael King 2005
Photographs copyright © Michael King 2005
except for those listed on page 192

Published in North America in 2005 by
Timber Press, Inc.
The Haseltine Building
133 S.W. Second Avenue, Suite 450
Portland, Oregon 97204-3527, U.S.A.
www.timberpress.com

ISBN 0-88192-744-9

A catalog record for this book is available
from the Library of Congress

Printed and bound in China

9 8 7 6 5 4 3 2 1

TITLE PAGE *Tulipa praestans* 'Van
Tubergen's Variety' (Miscellaneous)
with the Fosteriana Group tulip
'Madame Lefeber' in the
background
RIGHT Single Late Group tulip
'Blushing Lady'

CONTENTS

PREFACE

Until I came to live in Amsterdam, the capital of the Netherlands, I had not grown more than the occasional clump or pot of tulips in my London garden. In autumn tulip bulbs are for sale everywhere: the local petrol station, supermarkets and of course every garden centre. Like most people, I would grab a packet, tempted by the colour photograph of the promised flowers, and rarely was I disappointed. Even when I failed to get around to planting them until Christmas these easy-going bulbs lived up to their promise, flowering reliably every time.

The tulip, with its rich history, diversity and worldwide fame, has an identity crisis: it is too familiar and too easy to grow to be considered exclusive and desirable. 'If anyone can grow them, why bother?' is probably the attitude of many gardeners, who buy on impulse when reminded how beautiful they can be but never think of using them as a bold planting theme for their spring gardens.

Gardening is all about self-expression and making idiosyncratic choices which create outdoor spaces that we can call our own. Rose and herb gardens are inspired by romance and nostalgia and many a drift of golden daffodils has followed from Wordsworth's words. In my case, the cultural significance of the tulip to the Netherlands provided an impetus, especially when I recalled the days of madness in the seventeenth century when tulip mania rocked the economy – all this took place in the very streets and buildings I now called home. Yet even here in the Netherlands very few

gardeners seem to be inspired to grow more than a handful of tulips in their gardens.

In truth, today's market for tulips is dominated by the cut flower trade, with millions of flowers being sent worldwide every week of the year from the auction house in Aalsmeer, just outside Amsterdam. This multi-million-euro market is not the exclusive preserve of the Dutch, but their continued innovation and marketing abilities keeps them at the forefront of the industry. With only some 10 per cent of the bulbs produced in the Netherlands being sold for planting in gardens, the emphasis clearly lies on the production of bulbs for forcing as cut flowers.

This book aims to illustrate the many ways these bulbs can be used in contemporary gardens. I sketch their origins and history as a foundation to our appreciation, but above all else I emphasize their invaluable contribution to the spring garden scene in combinations with other bulbs, perennials, shrubs and trees. Throughout, I recommend only the very best tulips for use in gardens, avoiding those that have been developed solely for cut flower production and a few difficult-to-grow species that are best left to alpine plant enthusiasts. At this early stage, however, I should also issue a warning: an interest in growing tulips can very quickly turn into an obsession, and although they are relatively cheap to buy and easy to grow, only the size of your garden or bank account are likely to assert any form of effective control.

Michael King
Amsterdam 2005

Cut flowers gathered from my garden

INTRODUCTION

Some flowers, like people, stand out from the crowd. They are destined to become the stars, prima donnas and leaders in their society. Their status may come about through a combination of factors – physical size, beauty, talent or personality, or sometimes it is simply perseverance that gives them the edge.

Many other spring-flowering bulbs can fill the scene with colour – snowdrops, winter aconites and cyclamen are quickly followed by daffodils and bluebells – but all are at their best *en masse* spreading across garden borders, around the base of trees and in wide drifts across the garden landscape. In comparison, tulips stand out as individuals with sufficient presence to be used discretely in carefully assembled groupings that highlight their varied forms and colours. When tulips are massed together in park bedding schemes they lose this individuality and become a common tool for providing a splash of colour. Only by appreciating their unique qualities and exploiting them to the full can we expect to get the best out of any plant and sadly, all too often, the tulip's reputation has been damaged by its insensitive use. In part, it is its own worst enemy, being so easily grown and cheap to purchase that it encourages abuse and excess. Tulips are clearly plants for the foreground: bold and confident, they have the ability to rule their surroundings, stimulating our senses with colour, form and pattern, and thereby altering our mood and the atmosphere of the spaces they occupy.

What makes the tulip the star of our spring gardens is also the result of history, of beauty and poise, of breeding and above all of being in the right place at the right time and seizing every opportunity. The tulip has come a long way from its origins and this is where any appreciation of these truly remarkable plants must begin, but first we need to understand the finer details of its form and structure.

LEFT 'Temple of Beauty' – Single Late Group tulip

ANATOMY OF THE TULIP

As gardeners, we begin our acquaintance with tulips when they are bulbs. These normally arrive in net bags or brown-paper sacks with holes that allow the free circulation of air while the bulbs are out of the ground. The bulbs are covered in a smooth brown skin, the tunic, through which a white growing tip breaks, causing it to shatter and fall away. Breeders of tulips favour varieties with tough resilient tunics, as these help protect them during handling and transportation, but they are not essential for their well-being. The base of the bulb is flattened with corrugations around the edges, from which the first stages of root growth may be visible. Usually bulbs are slightly flattened on one side, on which can be found a small scar and possibly the remnants of the previous year's flower stem.

The bulbs of wild tulips vary considerably from the familiar garden hybrids both in size and shape, as can be seen in the illustration (left). Their tunics vary in colour, texture and thickness and may also be associated with a fluffy inner fibrous layer that can sometimes be seen protruding from their growing tip. Features such as these are particularly important to botanists trying to identify and classify the many wild tulip species. Likewise some species such as *Tulipa sylvestris* and *T. saxatilis* develop extension growths (stolons) from the base of the mother bulbs to spread their colonies sideways.

Mixed tulip bulbs – wild species and garden cultivars

In cross section, a bulb can be seen to be made up of four or five overlapping coats or layers enveloping a column that terminates in the growing tip. This column, arising from the base plate of the bulb, is the rudimentary flower, encased within incipient leaves. The small bud at its base will eventually develop into next year's bulb and in addition there may also be some small, offset, bulbs attached to the outside of the bulb's base.

When the bulb begins to grow, roots emerge from the base and subsequently the central column elongates until the growing point emerges from the soil. This extends, and then splits vertically to become a folded leaf that gradually begins to unravel. Simultaneously a second leaf unfolds, facing in the opposite direction, and from between them rises the central stalk, which terminates in the flower bud. The bulb that is not going to flower in the current year produces only one leaf. These are immature bulbs, possibly grown from seed or offsets, which have not yet built up enough strength to flower. In the tulip trade, these are termed widows.

As the stem grows longer, it develops two or three extra narrower leaves that become more pointed the higher up the stem they appear. Usually each stem carries a single flower, although there are a number of exceptions to this, as we will see later.

The tulip's flower is pure logic, which undoubtedly confers its simple refinement and

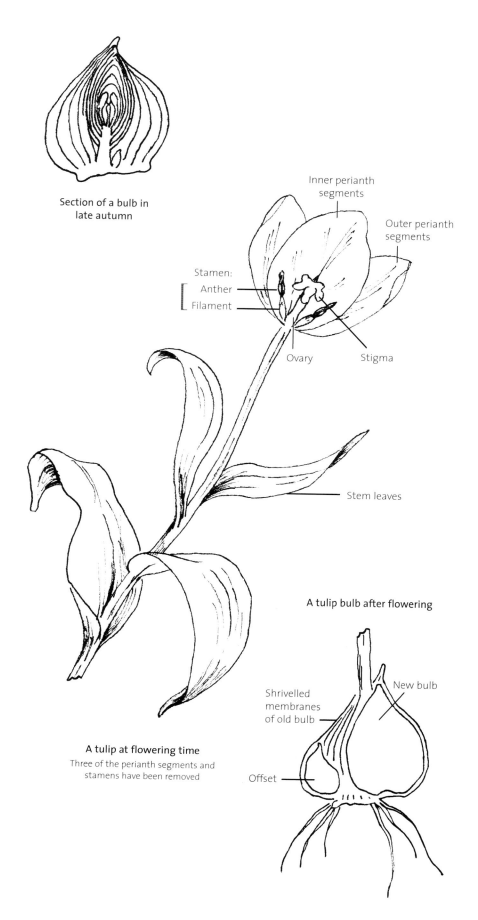

Section of a bulb in
late autumn

Inner perianth
segments

Outer perianth
segments

Stamen:

Anther

Filament

Ovary

Stigma

Stem leaves

A tulip bulb after flowering

Shrivelled
membranes
of old bulb

New bulb

Offset

A tulip at flowering time
Three of the perianth segments and
stamens have been removed

poise. There are six perianth segments or petals arranged in two sets of three, an inner and an outer, to form a symmetrical bowl. These two types of petals differ slightly from one another in shape: the outer three are generally broader at the base and more rounded, and the inner petals are much narrower at the base and consequently more wedge-shaped.

Within the perianth there are six stamens consisting of long filaments arising from the base of the flowers, which narrow towards their tips as they connect, endwise, to large anthers. The stamens surround a thick triangular ovary, which is terminated by a stigmatic surface for the reception of pollen. There is no style present, although in some cases there is a suggestion of one with a constriction at the top of the ovary just underneath the stigma. The stigma varies greatly in size and in its pattern of convolutions and, like all other elements of the flower, may exhibit different colouration from the rest.

Garden tulips are self-fertile, although the stigmatic surface does not become receptive to pollen for two or three days after the flowers open. This mechanism is common in the plant world and may help increase the likelihood of cross-fertilization with other plants, which in the case of the tulip could be other garden cultivars or species of tulip. Following fertilization the ovary takes eight to ten weeks to ripen, whereupon it splits along its three

Tulipa sprengeri seed pod
(Miscellaneous)

From seed, a modern tulip takes between five and seven years to flower. Each year a new bulb is formed, a process that is reflected in the number of overlapping coats or layers within the mature bulb. The exceptions to this are a few species tulips with smaller bulbs that may flower in as few as three years from seed. In the wild, the bulbs of species tulips grow deep in the soil. This is made possible when stoloniferous growths appear from the base of the mother bulb and grow downwards before forming a new bulb at their tips. These structures are called droppers and are a common feature of immature tulips being grown from seed. Droppers form each year, relocating the immature bulbs deeper and deeper in the soil, and by the time they are large enough to flower they will be positioned deep below the soil's surface.

The process of mother bulbs generating daughter bulbs and offsets is the method by which modern-day tulip cultivars are produced in millions. In theory one would imagine that the process could continue indefinitely; however practice shows that after maybe many years the clones begin to lose their vigour, grow poorly and eventually die out. This ageing process is by no means fully understood and cannot be predicted. Some tulip cultivars have succumbed in less than thirty years while at the same time we still have a number of very old clones such as 'Keizerskroon' (*c*.1750) and 'Zomerschoon' (*c*.1620), which show no signs of ageing.

Although tulips can also be increased from seed, only the true species produce offspring resembling their parents. Modern tulips are the result of centuries of cross-breeding. The seed produced by cross-breeding results in tulips in many shapes and colours, nearly all of which are inferior to their parents, but for the tulip breeder with patience and a good eye this can be a way of finding new cultivars for the future with different colours, improved form or greater vigour.

Even the seedlings of species tulips can exhibit wide variability, creating wild populations with wide variations in both shape

edges to reveal neatly stacked rows of seeds. These are rich brown in colour and thin, flat and triangular in shape, with their embryo as a swelling clearly visible near to one of the corners. Gardeners are likely to remove the flowers before this stage in order to conserve the plant's energy and redirect it into the formation of next year's bulb.

Digging up a tulip after it has flowered will reveal a remarkable transformation. The original bulb will have shrivelled into a bundle of dead skins, but a new bulb will have developed adjacent to the old flower stem. The new bulb arises from the internal bud growing near the base of the mother bulb and its flattened side results from the way it is pushed up against the flower stem as it develops. (Incidentally, immature bulbs that fail to flower produce round symmetrical new bulbs.) Additionally there may be offset bulbs that have developed from dormant buds on the base plate of the mother bulb. Depending upon their size, these will grow into flowering bulbs in one or two years' time.

'Synaeda Blue' (Triumph)

and the colouration of their flowers. Here we are confronted with the true character of the tulip, and something that causes expert taxonomists and botanists many problems. In the past individual bulbs have been sent to the West, where botanists have given them unique specific names, only to discover much later that they are merely variations of one species. This confusion continues to the present day as attempts are made to unravel the relationships and evolution of the various wild species. As gardeners this need not concern us unduly; however, it does shed light upon our appreciation of how ingenious and successful the tulip has been through the centuries in firing the imagination of enthusiastic collectors and adapting its character to contemporary tastes. Unlike most other plants, tulips are unstable and unpredictable. Even when sex is removed from the equation and they are propagated from bulbs, mutations – the so-called sports – regularly occur. These may exhibit a change in flower colour, a doubling in the number of petals or an

alteration in the shape of the flower or its petals. The ability of apparently stable selections to throw up sports has been one of the most significant ways in which new cultivars have been acquired. The tulip's wild nature to change and adapt cannot be tamed and this allows it to continuously alter and offer tantalizing glimpses of new possibilities.

It is not often realized that many tulip flowers are scented. Species such as *T. sylvestris* and *T. humilis* are sweetly scented when encountered at close quarters, growing in a pot for instance. Likewise, the Double Early tulip 'Monte Carlo' and its many sports such as 'Abba' and 'Monsella', which are grown in large numbers for the cut flower trade, plus old favourites like Single Early 'Apricot Beauty' and 'Generaal de Wet' and Lily-flowered 'Ballerina', are all strongly scented. Beetles, bees and other insects have all been observed visiting the flowers, and presumably scent together with vivid flower colours have evolved as mechanisms to attract them. Needless to say, flower colour is the primary

'Big Chief' (Darwinhybrid)

'West Point' (Lily-flowered)

'Prins Carnaval' (Single Early)

Tulipa sprengeri (Miscellaneous)

reason we as gardeners grow tulips today. However, scent is an added attraction: it is the strong scent of 'Ballerina', for example, that has long been my justification for growing it alongside one of the paths in my own garden.

Tulip flowers are rarely of a single pure colour. The inside colour can differ from the outer colour, which itself may be overlaid by other colours in patterns such as flames spreading from the centre outwards or streaks and splashes. A flame of pale yellow, pink or purple is very common and, where the streaking is gathered towards the edge of the petals, it can create a feather-like pattern.

Inside, the base of the petals may have a different colour; white and yellow are common, as is jet black. These basal markings may themselves be edged in contrasting colours, most commonly yellow, and may further be overlaid with blotches or regular coloured patterns in blue, green, brown or other muddy tones. On the outside, the flower colour may vary towards the base, sometimes becoming pale, even fading to white, and quite often it is yellow. The extent to which we are aware of these various features depends upon the age of the flower and whether it is fully open or in the closed bud stage. Many tulips open widely in sunshine to reveal their basal marks while in other cases such variations play a less important role in their general appearance.

The colour of a tulip flower is determined in the main by the interaction of two groups of pigments. Firstly, there is a ground colour, white or yellow, situated in the cells forming the main body of the petals, the mesophyll. Above this is a thin layer of cells forming a cuticle that may contain a water-soluble sap colour, an anthocyanin, of various shades of crimson and purple. In pure yellow- and pure white-flowered tulips the anthocyanins may be absent; in other cases, their presence in various combinations and intensities determines the final flower colour as they are modified by the underlying ground colour. The science need not bother us further, but what is important to grasp is the fact that two sets of pigments create the colours we see, and the effect varies

depending upon how light falls upon the flowers. When a flower is lit from behind, the ground colour shines brightly through the overlying cuticle layer; when the light shines on to the front of a flower, the pigments in its cuticle layer have more effect and the colour we see is different. Even before I understood the reason for the effect, I was aware that many tulips looked at their best when lit from behind and that some were positively ugly when directly lit. In theory, therefore, backlighting should not make any difference to pure white and yellow tulips, but for all others it will reveal the true richness and complexity of their colouring.

In addition to a yellow pigment in the mesophyll, there can be a yellow pigment present in the cuticle layer. The effect of this is to give a warm yellow blush to the petals, but it is quickly broken down by strong sunlight, which can account for some tulips gradually changing colour within the first few days of opening their flowers. Conversely, certain varieties open with a fine tracery of anthocyanin pigment, which gradually spreads all over their petals as they age. Possibly the finest example of this in our current assortment is the Single Late tulip 'Magier', whose fresh white flowers are initially lightly traced in violet blue but eventually become saturated with this rich pigmentation.

A feature of some species tulips is the tendency for the backs of the three outer petals to be a different colour from the colour of their inside surfaces and both the inside and outside surfaces of the three inner petals. This results in the sort of flower possessed by *Tulipa sprengeri*, which when closed appears dull metallic bronze, but once touched by sunshine opens to reveal a vividly glowing crimson centre. The exquisite *T. clusiana* is another: pure white apart from a broad carmine red mark on the backs of its three outer petals.

Descriptions of flower colour appear throughout this book. Terms such as flames, feathers, streaks and splashes help describe colour effects, but to fully appreciate the beauty of a flower, you also need to search for

other subtleties that it exhibits. Is the colour uniform or is there a difference between the colour on the inside and on the outside? Base colours can be exquisite, from white through shades of brown and bronze to black and blue. Are they edged in a contrasting colour or do they bear overlying blotches? Are they confined to the inside of the flower or are they repeated on the outside as well? Pollen comes in a range of colours from black to purple and yellow and the anthers may be borne on filaments in contrasting tones of green, yellow or red. The ovary is normally green, but the stigmatic surface at its tip may be green, yellow or white. Knowing what to look for is the key to enjoying these flowers. Not only does it reveal their subtle beauty to you; it also offers an insight into the minds of those who have become enraptured by tricks and turns of the unpredictable tulip throughout its long and colourful history.

'Lighting Sun' and 'Negrita', lit from behind (Darwinhybrid/Triumph)

Tulipa acuminata (Miscellaneous)

ORIGIN AND HISTORY OF GARDEN TULIPS

The name tulip is incorrect. In fact, it should be *lalé*, the Turkish name for the flower endemic to the region and once synonymous with the culture of the Ottoman Empire. The mistake was made by Ogier Ghiselin de Busbecq (1522–92), who earned his place in history as allegedly being the first Westerner to encounter the tulip and as the man who introduced it into Europe. His record of his journey to Constantinople in 1554 is where the erroneous name first surfaces. He recounts how 'We were going on towards Constantinople, now near, for we were almost accomplishing the end of our journey, and as we were passing through a district an abundance of flowers was everywhere offered to us – Narcissus, Hyacinths, and those which the Turks call *tulipam* … Scent in tulips is wanting or very slight; they are admired for the variety and beauty of their colours. The Turks cultivate flowers with extreme zeal, and though they are careful people, do not hesitate to pay a considerable sum for an exceptional flower.' The name *tulipam* or tulip is clearly the result of a mix-up. The only word in Turkish for a tulip is *lâle*; *tülband* is the Turkish form of the Persian *dulband*, referring to the cloth used to create their traditional headdress, the fez or turban. Busbecq's interpreter must have used the word *tülband* either to compare the shape of the tulip to a turban or, more likely, because it was common practice at the time to decorate the turban by slipping a tulip between its folds.

Home and habitat

The tulip's origins lie in the East. The line of latitude 40° north traces a band of distribution from the far north-west of China across to Turkey covering some of the world's most inaccessible and inhospitable mountainous regions. Some 40 per cent of known species have been found growing within a 620 mile/1,000 kilometre radius of west Tien Shan and the Pamir Alai mountain ranges, which seems to suggest that this was the genetic centre for the genus *Tulipa*. From here the tulip spread north and eastwards in the direction of China, Siberia and Mongolia, southwards towards Kashmir and India, and westwards through Afghanistan, Iran, Iraq and the Caucasus. On reaching the Caucasus, it apparently found the growing conditions to its liking, as this became a second genetic centre, with 20 per cent of known species originating here. From this new stronghold it spread further westwards, across Turkey and the Black Sea to the Balkans, Greece, Romania and Hungary. It edged its way around the southern shores of the Mediterranean Sea through Lebanon, Israel, the islands of Cyprus and Crete and even as far as Algeria and Morocco. *Tulipa australis*, appearing at the limit of the tulip's spread, is found growing wild both in the Sierra Nevada in southern Spain as well as across the sea in Morocco and Algeria. Occurrences of tulips as far west as Italy, France and Switzerland cannot always be attributed to its natural distribution as in these locations the species found are clearly of hybrid origin and are typically associated with cultivated land. This far from their homeland, tulips were clearly being spread and influenced by the hand of man.

Knowing its origins helps us understand the tulip's needs. What seem to us to be inhospitable mountain slopes strewn with rock and dust, scorched in summer and bitterly cold in winter, are home to the ancestors of garden tulips. The nearer we come to mirroring these conditions in our gardens, the more successful we will be in growing tulips and increasing their number. Apparently, sunlight, heat, perfect drainage and cold winters make up the winning formula.

Human influences

To the nomadic tribes of Central Asia the first flowers of spring must have been a welcome signal marking the end of the extreme weather conditions of their winter. Crossing the Tien Shan mountain range via high-level passes to reach rich grazing pastures to the south, Turkish nomads would have been familiar with brightly coloured tulips, their impact no doubt intensified by the desolate conditions of their surroundings. Not surprisingly, here on the roof

'Furuzende' from *The Book of Tulips, c.*1725

Tulipa schrenkii
(Miscellaneous)

of the Earth the tulip came to symbolize birth, life, fertility and hope in the minds of those who shared its home.

Persian writers had been venerating the tulip long before the Turks began to establish permanent settlements and, with their Ottoman Empire, spread their influence westwards following a similar route taken by the tulip thousands of years earlier, across Asia and into Europe. Verses used tulips as a metaphor for female beauty, one poet, Hefig, going as far as to liken the sheen of their petals to the bloom on his mistress's cheeks. The tulip came to symbolize eternity and undying passion in Persia and was used as such in their gardens, which were an attempt to recreate paradise on Earth.

The Turks' gardens also became a symbol of heaven, filled with the things that were most precious to people living in a desert. The tulip, which had long been a steadfast travelling companion, became an essential component. There was no more holy flower, its name *lāle* using the same combination of Arabic letters as for the Turks' god, Allah.

In 1453, the Turks under Mehmed II (1432–81) conquered Constantinople. Renamed Istanbul, it became the capital of the Ottoman Empire, which flourished for the next three hundred years. Islam prohibited the

Tulipa acuminata
(Miscellaneous)

depiction of all living things, above all man. It was not until the relaxation of these rules around the beginning of the sixteenth century that the tulip began to be depicted, the flower's simple form lending itself to the symmetrical patterns that typified Islamic art.

Shortly after conquering Constantinople, Mehmed II (who was sultan from 1451) initiated the construction of his magnificent Topkapi Palace, which he referred to as the 'Abode of Bliss'. It was built to impress and subjugate all who entered it and at its heart, shielded from the eyes of visitors, was a garden with magnificent views across the Bosphorus. These gardens were extensive. Plants, especially tulips, were gathered from all over the empire to adorn its slopes and it is possible that the prized Istanbul tulips were given pride of place in the flower beds nearest to the Sultan's private quarters.

Süleyman the Magnificent, the great-grandson of Mehmed, came to the throne in 1520. During his reign, the Ottoman Empire was at its most powerful and extensive. It was at this time that the Turks began to breed tulips rather than just gather them from the wild, and by 1630 apparently there were eight flower shops and 300 professional florists in Istanbul.

Wild species such as *Tulipa schrenkii* have wide cup-shaped flowers, but the Turkish taste selected flowers with long, slender petals. Their ideal became varieties shaped like almonds with fine, needle-sharp pointed petals. These new hybrids were presumably the result of crossings of the many different species that were being brought back to the capital with each successive expansion of the empire. They were given evocative names such as Light of Paradise, Increaser of Pleasure, Instiller of Passion, Rose of Dawn and so on. Such flowers were scarce and highly prized by the court and its officials.

In the mid-sixteenth century the Ottoman Empire had won a string of victories in the Mediterranean, capturing Rhodes in 1522, entering Hungary in 1526 and three years later besieging Vienna. Christian monarchs were forced to negotiate with the Turks and possibly their envoys and ambassadors first encountered the tulip in Istanbul. Merchants and mercenaries would also

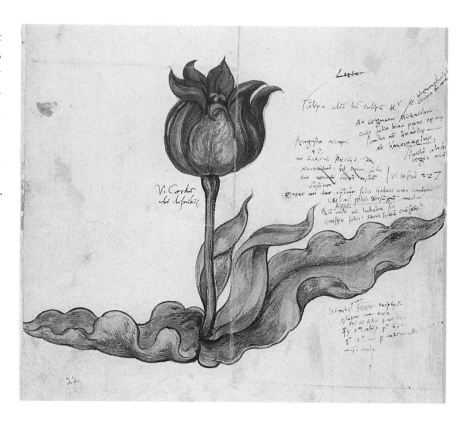

The first Western illustration of a tulip by Gesner, 1561

have found their way to Istanbul at this time, thereby gradually breaking down the barriers between East and West that had existed until then.

By whatever means the tulip crossed this divide, it was definitely growing in Europe by 1559, when the Zurich-based physician Conrad Gesner (1516–65) saw it flower in the garden of Johann Heinrich Herwart in Augsburg, Bavaria. Using the sketches he made at the time, Gesner made the first-ever Western image of the tulip, published in 1561.

In Turkey, the passion for tulips nurtured by Süleyman and later his son Selim II declined around the end of the sixteenth century with the accession of Mehmed III in 1595. It was not until 1647, when Mehmed IV became sultan, that the tulip regained royal favour. He restored the imperial gardens and decreed that all new species of flower should be registered and classified, and he established a council of florists to judge all new tulip cultivars.

The tulip in Europe

While Busbecq wrote the first European reference to the tulip and Gesner published the first illustration, it now seems likely that tulip

ABOVE 'Zomerschoon', c.1620 (Single Late)

BELOW Clusius's commemorative garden in the Hortus Botanicus, Leiden, the Netherlands

bulbs and seeds had found their way to European gardens before then; and they, like their reputation, quickly spread. Their most notorious proponent was the Frenchman Charles de l'Escluse, better known as Carolus Clusius (1526–1609). Busbecq sent bulbs and seeds back to Vienna. In 1572 Clusius met him and received a lot of seed and bulbs, which seems to have been his first encounter with the plant. Clusius was employed to establish the Imperial Botanic Gardens in Vienna, where he became familiar with these new rarities and eagerly exchanged them with correspondents throughout Europe. He was especially interested in bulbs and was responsible not only for

distributing tulips but also for many other new introductions such as anemones, crown imperials, hyacinths, irises, lilies and narcissi.

Auspiciously, at the age of sixty-seven, Clusius was persuaded to go to Leiden in the Netherlands in order to set up a physic garden for the newly established university there. He arrived in October 1593 and brought with him his collection of tulip bulbs. They were not the first tulips to flower in the Netherlands; however, the display at the new physic garden attracted a great deal of attention. On numerous occasions he was asked if he would sell some bulbs, but invariably he refused or asked an exorbitant price. For him they were ostensibly objects for study and for exchange with other academics. Inevitably one night his whole collection was stolen, which for Clusius was the final straw, and he lost heart and gave up growing them. However, those who acquired them lost no time in growing on the bulbs and their seeds until in a very short time tulips were widely distributed throughout the Low Countries. Simultaneously the commercial production of tulips in Europe began.

Tulip mania

Tulips became popular with royalty and the wealthy, in particular forms with flowers streaked and splashed with contrasting colours. A thriving trade developed around the city of Haarlem in the Netherlands where the sandy soils were well suited to their cultivation. This was a time of great prosperity. The Dutch East India Company was established in 1602 and demand for the most exquisite forms of tulip grew. The result was the best-chronicled and yet least significant period in tulip history. Between 1637 and the end of 1639 the so-called tulip mania (often referred to as tulipomania) ran its short course. The market in the most famous bulbs ran out of control as people from all levels of Dutch society became involved speculating in tulip bulbs. Fortunes were being made and everyone wanted a slice of the action. In reality, the quantity of bulbs was very small, and because of a virus infection they barely grew or increased in number. Few of those involved in the market were actually interested in

growing the plants and inevitably the whole house of cards collapsed as one after the other investor attempted to realize their profits.

The economic crisis in the Netherlands caused by tulip mania did not bring an end to the popularity of the tulip as is often assumed. Tulips continued to attract passionate gardeners and took pride of place in many a nobleman's collection. France was also a major player in the commercial tulip trade and in a way the scandal surrounding the Dutch crisis stimulated interest in the bulbs in other countries. Quantities were never huge but the assortment was extensive and consequently prices were high; only the wealthiest in society could afford to grow them in quantity.

Fashions and florists

In the 1660s, Louis XIV held extravagant parties, filling the Grand Trianon at Versailles with tulips, narcissi and hyacinths. His successor Louis XV favoured exotics not tulips. In the early eighteenth century the French built up a profitable export trade with England, Holland and Germany. In England, seventeenth-century gardens peaked in spring and early summer, as there were very few late-flowering plants available. The tulip was deemed essential in every gentleman's garden, where formal designs allowed them to be planted in neat grid patterns, facilitating the easy recording of names of the individual jewels in their costly collections.

By the 1730s tastes had changed in England. Glasshouses containing tender exotics became popular. Trees and shrubs from America started to arrive and Lancelot 'Capability' Brown (1716–83) began to replace formality with his new landscape style. Following the Seven Years War, French things became unpopular and at the time this also meant the tulip.

Throughout the eighteenth century, however, although the hyacinth rose to top of the popularity charts, the tulip trade continued, and the region around Lille in northern France became a major centre of production. By the nineteenth century, tastes in tulips seemed to change away from subtle variations in petal form and colour to simpler early-blooming single-coloured tulips. It seemed as if society in the new

industrialized era required standardized, mass-produced tulips. As Europe found peace and prosperity in the second half of the nineteenth century, the demand for garden flowers increased within all levels of society, as did an interest in cut flowers. Greenhouses for the production of tulips sprang up around most major European cities and the demand for single and double early varieties exploded. Improved communications aided the export trade, and Britain, ruled by Queen Victoria, and subsequently America became major importers of Dutch and French tulips. The tulip, which had once been reserved for sultans and kings, was now destined to become the people's flower.

Herman Henstenburgh (1667–1726), *Three Tulips*, Teylers Museum, Haarlem

Broken colouration of a virus-infected tulip

In England, as in France and Turkey, whenever fashion turned away from the tulip it never truly disappeared, since there were always those who loved it and continued to breed and improve it; such artisans, termed florists, were the tradespeople of their time. With little money but great skill and patience, they strove over time to perfect their flowers to conform to strict criteria. For example, between 1750 and 1850 nearly every town in the north of England held a tulip show, but here also fashions changed and by the end of the nineteenth century only one society remained; dahlias and chrysanthemums had become the florists' new passions. Nevertheless, their future was secure, as by this time tulips had become items to satisfy the mass market as cut flowers and bulbs for public park bedding displays.

The tulip virus

Up to the end of the nineteenth century, the forms of tulip that had flower petals streaked, flamed or feathered in rich and subtle colours were the most prized. These patterns arose spontaneously and unpredictably in newly bred bulbs, which in the first few years of their lives had produced pure, evenly coloured flowers that had at some point 'broken', with the result that the original colour was no longer evenly spread over the petal but concentrated into lines and stripes, leaving other areas paler or showing only the clear yellow or white base colour of their petal's mesophyll. Once established, the exotically patterned plants could be propagated from their bulbs and the pattern of breaking remained consistent. New varieties were created by crossing the unbroken tulips that made up a florist's or nurseryman's breeding stock, and these tulips were termed breeders.

Many theories were suggested to explain the phenomenon of breaking and many practices were tried to initiate it in breeder tulips. It was noted that broken tulips lacked the vigour and vitality of their breeder forms, and by the beginning of the twentieth century some form of infection was suspected as being the cause. It was not until 1928 that Dorothy Cayley (1874–1955), a mycologist at the John Innes Horticultural Institute in Merton near London, finally confirmed this by isolating the tulip breaking virus (TBV).

By the time of the virus's discovery, single pure-coloured tulips were needed in vast numbers for park bedding schemes and the cut flower trade. The old-fashioned forms with their weak constitutions had been superseded and now that it was seen that they carried disease they were quickly banished from commercial production. Today the tulip virus is a constant threat to the prosperity of the tulip industry and it is ruthlessly controlled and eliminated.

Modern-day tulips

Today's tulips were born out of the change that occurred during the middle of the nineteenth century when tulips became the subject of massed bedding displays in public gardens and ceased to be seen as single exquisite items of beauty. The trend started in America when, for example, in 1845, 600 different sorts were bedded out in the Linnaean Botanic Gardens on Long Island. Initially early-flowering brightly coloured varieties would probably have been used such as 'Couleur Cardinal' (1845) and the double 'Murillo' (1860). Production in the Netherlands increased to supply the growing

demand. The nurseryman E.H. Krelage was quick to pick up on this new trend and had a significant influence on the development of modern-day tulips when in 1889 he introduced his new tall later-flowering Darwin tulips.

As florists lost interest in tulips, Krelage bought up the last of the great French collections from M. Jules Lenglart of Lille. He discarded the broken forms and selected the best of the pure-coloured breeders. These were robust, vigorous plants with broad, substantial petals that made round cup-shaped flowers with a distinctive square profile. The stems were long and sturdy, enabling them to stand up to rain and wind, and held the flowers at a height where they could be appreciated from the side and at a distance, thus making Darwin tulips ideal for mass bedding.

In England, as interest in florists' tulips dwindled, the nurseryman Peter Barr, like Krelage, set about buying up the old varieties and trying to promote them as ideal for garden usage. However, the tulips lacked the vigour of those found by Krelage in France and were unable to compete with the new range of Darwin tulips he had developed from them. Peter Barr also sought tulip varieties in old gardens where country people had grown them for decades. Their origins were obscure: some would have been grown from seed or acquired as cast-offs from gentlemen's prized collections, or maybe they were rejected florists' breeders. The fact that they had survived confirmed their ability to cope with garden conditions and many of these so-called cottage tulips eventually found their way into commercial production.

To satisfy the new taste for cut flowers, in 1921 Krelage introduced yet another new group of tulips called Mendel tulips. These were an attempt to create a long-stemmed tulip suitable for forcing as cut flowers early in the season. He crossed the Darwin tulips with an old race of Dutch tulips called Duc van Tol hybrids which were popular as they could be forced into flower before Christmas but unfortunately were small and short growing; by crossing them with the Darwins, the aim was to overcome this weakness. These were in their turn popular for some time, but they were not the sturdiest of tulips. Some Mendel tulips are still with us today, such as the ever-popular 'Apricot Beauty', but as a group they were superseded by the newer, stronger-growing Triumph tulips.

Triumph tulips were created by crossing Single Early tulips with mid- and late-season tulips with the express aim of creating sturdy bedding tulips that might have the added ability to be suitable for forcing as cut flowers. They dominate present-day production and are the quintessential modern tulip.

In the 1940s, following the discoveries of new wild species, D.W. Lefeber made crosses between *Tulipa fosteriana* and some of Krelage's old Darwin tulips to create the perfect park bedding tulips, the Darwinhybrids. These tulips with their huge square-shaped flowers atop thick long stems quickly overran traffic islands and roadsides the world over.

Today's assortment continues to develop along the same lines with tulip breeders searching for improvements in colour, flower shape and disease resistance. Increasingly the emphasis is on new varieties for the cut flower trade, but many of these newer introductions also prove to be good garden plants. Today's assortment therefore embodies the best of the tulip's past with growers' aspirations for it to remain one of the most popular garden plants in the future.

Classification of garden tulips

By the beginning of the twentieth century the naming of new tulip cultivars was completely out of hand, with the same names being used for more than one tulip and some having different names in different countries and/or growers' catalogues. In 1913 the Royal Horticultural Society in England decided to set up a committee with the assistance of the Dutch to sort out their naming and the classification. In 1914 the Tulip Nomenclature Committee sat for the first time with the famous bulb expert

E.A. Bowles as its chairman and the Dutch grower E.H. Krelage as its vice-chairman. Trials were undertaken at Wisley in 1915 using bulbs requisitioned from Dutch and English growers and in 1917 their first report appeared in spite of the fact that the Dutch members of the committee had been unable to attend meetings because of travel restrictions imposed during the First World War. The report gave a long list of synonyms to be eliminated and proposed a classification in which fourteen groups of tulips were organized into early-flowering and May-flowering sections.

Subsequently classified lists of tulip names have been issued in which new cultivars have been recorded and the classification has been refined. In 1955 the KAVB (Koninklijke Algemeene Vereeniging voor Bloembollencultuur/ Royal General Bulb Growers' Association) in the Netherlands became the international registration authority for tulips and since that time it has issued revised editions of the Classified List and International Register of Tulip Names, the latest being published in 1996.

The correct names of wild species tulips continue to challenge taxonomists. In this book I use the names as given in the KAVB list, although current research indicates that some revisions are needed. When this is the case I have also given updated names. However internationally the old names will continue to appear in bulb trade lists and catalogues while we await a revised edition of the official list.

From the earliest days, tulips have been recognized as falling into one of three categories: early-, mid-season- and late-flowering varieties. The current classification goes much further than this with fifteen groups reflecting to some extent the respective flowering times of the tulips, but also bringing together similarities of flower form and pedigree. The classification begins logically with the Single Early and Double Early Groups up to the Double Late Group. Three groups of so-called Botanical tulips follow, which are respectively the species and similar-looking hybrids of *T. kaufmanniana*, *T. fosteriana* and *T. greigii*. The final, Miscellaneous group gathers together all other wild species and their cultivars. The Botanical tulips and the species span the full spectrum of flowering times with some Kaufmanniana Group and Miscellaneous species being amongst the very first to flower with Fosteriana and then Greigii Group tulips following in their turn along with the remaining members of the Miscellaneous group.

The Duc van Tol cultivars, which were important for early forcing, were initially allocated their own group, but when the Mendel Group and subsequently Triumph Group tulips superseded them they became subsumed into the Single Early Group. In turn, as the Mendel tulips diminished in importance those of them that remained in production were reclassified as either Single Early or Triumph tulips depending upon their flowering times. Likewise Darwin tulips were initially given their own group in the classification, but these were eventually overshadowed by their progeny, the Darwinhybrids. Consequently, Darwin tulips were combined with the old cottage and florists' breeder tulips into a new group called Single Late tulips in 1981, but any with green-striped or fringed-petalled flowers were placed into new groups for Viridiflora and Fringed tulips. For

First Tulip Classification – 1917	Current Tulip Classification – 1996
Early flowering 1 Duc van Tol 2 Single Early 3 Double Early **May flowering** 4 Cottage 5 Dutch Florist 6 English Florist 7 Darwin 8 Broken Dutch 9 Broken English 10 Rembrandt 11 Broken Cottage 12 Parrot 13 Late Double 14 Species	**Early flowering** 1 Single Early Group 2 Double Early Group **Mid-season** 3 Triumph Group 4 Darwinhybrid Group **Late** 5 Single Late Group 6 Lily-flowered Group 7 Fringed Group 8 Viridiflora Group 9 Rembrandt Group 10 Parrot Group 11 Double Late Group **Species** 12 Kaufmanniana Group 13 Fosteriana Group 14 Greigii Group 15 Miscellaneous

historical reasons a group termed Rembrandt Group tulips has been retained within the current classification. These are broken, virus-infected cultivars which are no longer in production but can still be encountered in historical collections.

Bulb field, Lisse, the Netherlands

TULIPS IN CONTEMPORARY GARDENS

Beauty is in the eye of the beholder, but most people seem to agree that the simple rounded form of a tulip flower is elegant. Its six petals create a distinctive flower with a clean profile that can vary from a bird's-egg-shaped bud to an open cup. Some flowers bear petals reflexed outwards towards their tips, which affords them a sinuous grace, even sensuality. Purity of form seems to me to be an essential characteristic for a tulip flower. This explains why I am less excited by double-flowered tulips which, although bold colourful plants, can present a heavy, muddled appearance.

While historical associations may well be a strong motivation for choosing to grow certain tulips, the simple shapes and clear colours of tulips can also make references to modern design style. The uniformity presented by a bunch of pure red 'Ile de France' tulips, for example, makes them the ideal material to create a minimalist flower arrangement, crammed neatly into a simple upright vase. This holds true in the garden as well, when uniform blocks or lines of tulips are bedded out in bold geometric patterns. The uniformity that makes these severe designs succeed comes in part from the rigorous standardization of today's production systems which ensures that each bulb produces flowers of exactly the same size, height and colour. This, coupled with the tulip's slim upright form and long sturdy stem, can create displays as rigid as anything to be seen on a military parade ground.

Why choose tulips?

Having accepted that tulips are beautiful enough to earn a place in our gardens and easy plants to organize into different forms of display, there are two overriding reasons why we should decide to grow them. Firstly, they flower early in the year and are one of the first groups of plants that are capable of making a bold display to bring the garden alive after its winter rest, and secondly, they offer a wide spectrum of vibrant colours.

Colour is probably the main reason tulips are grown today. Mass bedding schemes, where emphasis lies more upon the total colour effect than the individual beauty of single flowers, are far from being the only way we can use them; even as small groups or in pots in our gardens, their colours will probably be foremost in our minds when we select the individual cultivars we grow.

Beyond pure aesthetic considerations, a number of other reasons for growing specific cultivars can be identified. For me the tulip's status in the culture of the Ottoman Empire is fascinating and this inspires me to grow *Tulipa acuminata* and many Lily-flowered cultivars that recall images of the lyre-shaped Istanbul tulips once so popular. The stories surrounding the tulip mania in seventeenth-century Holland

LEFT 'Kingsblood'
(Single Late)

'Abu Hassan' (Triumph)

may lead to a search for Rembrandt Group tulips or at least modern-day cultivars with feather-patterned petals resembling those that were once so prized.

A link with the past can also be made by growing some of the oldest cultivars still in today's assortment. 'Zomerschoon' is known from 1620, some thirty years before the start of tulip mania, and 'Keizerskroon', which has vigorously feathered red and yellow petals, dates from 1750. 'Prince of Austria' is a fine old Single Early cultivar dating from 1860, from which the highly desirable sport 'Generaal de Wet' arose. The assembly of lineages of tulip families can become an absorbing aspect of collecting tulips and lead to pleasing aesthetic associations. When a tulip produces a sport the new cultivar will often bear many similarities to its parent, almost invariably growing to the same size and flowering at the same time. Often, by mixing these parents with their offspring you can achieve pleasing harmonious associations.

Tulips have been given names to commemorate many different things and by association these might also provide an excuse to grow them. Family names and the names of friends may be tracked down and the bulbs grown out of nostalgia or love. Some cultivars have been named after companies and businessmen: 'Alfred Heineken' is a fine Pils-coloured Triumph tulip. The names of film stars, musicians and composers have all been used and many members of royalty immortalized, all of which can become reasons to grow the tulips bearing their names. Likewise, place names are common. I might choose to grow 'Amsterdam', a bright red Triumph, if the mood takes me. The Classified List of Tulip Names runs to more than 2,600 entries, offering endless possibilities, although actually acquiring the cultivars may not always be too easy.

Species tulips might also be an area that the collector turns to with enthusiasm as here are to be found some exquisite gems. Many will be too small for the open garden but can become highly rewarding subjects around the edges of a rock garden or in pots inside the alpine greenhouse.

Why you choose to grow tulips will be down to you, but the one thing they all have in common is their ability to please. I can think of no other plant that comes with such a high probability of success. A freshly purchased bulb planted in the autumn is virtually guaranteed to flower on time the following spring. The planting schemes we imagine become satisfying reality just six months later; compare that with most other garden features, which can take years to reach maturity.

USING TULIPS IN THE GARDEN

The least obvious but an extremely convenient place to grow tulips is the vegetable plot. Here there is room to provide them with ideal growing conditions: an open situation, free from shade and competition, and soil that is friable, fertile and freely draining. This is where we can cosset the immature offset bulbs of those special tulips that we want to retain in our garden displays but are rarely offered for sale. Many varieties lacking the vigour to reappear reliably in garden borders can be kept going in this way, thereby saving the expense of repurchasing them every couple of years. Following the methods of the commercial growers, let them come into flower to check their names and to rogue out any showing signs of the tulip breaking virus before removing the flowers and so directing all their energies into the formation of a new and larger bulb. Growing in rows, they are easily lifted for storage in the summer months, and will usually reach flowering size within two or three seasons of such treatment.

The vegetable plot is also the ideal place to grow tulips for cutting without having to plunder border displays for flowers for use inside the house. The effort involved in planting tulip bulbs in rows and gathering their flowers in spring is minimal. The great advantage is that you can plan and grow exactly the colours and varieties that most appeal to you without having to hope that your local florist will be offering them when spring comes round. Not everyone is as lucky as I am to live within walking distance of Amsterdam's famous flower market, which offers upwards of thirty sorts of tulip, different each day, throughout winter and spring and even a few in the height of summer.

Tulips in pots

Not every gardener has enough space for a separate vegetable plot and many of us have nothing more than a small patio or balcony to work with. A few pots of tulips are the perfect way to bring alive such spaces in spring – typically empty and dull throughout the winter. Nothing could be easier than to fill a few pots with compost and bulbs in the autumn and leave the rest to nature, but it does require a little planning. Of course, the garden centres will have done the work for us and in spring we can buy ready-grown pots of bulbs for an instant display, but, again, the choice will be extremely limited.

Tulips can always be mixed with other bulbs and spring-flowering plants in containers to create elaborate displays. Personally, I prefer to keep the design simple, using just a single variety per container either on its own or in association with a less dominant, complementary companion such as ground-cover ivy, pale blue forget-me-nots (*Myosotis*), pansies (*Viola*) or wallflowers (*Erysimum*). On a patio and

'Early Harvest' (Kaufmanniana)

'Dordogne' (Single Late)

to a lesser extent on a balcony, a pot filled with colourful tulips will create a focal point. Restraint is called for, as within such confined spaces too many pots and too many different varieties can very quickly turn what should be a sophisticated display into a riot of colour.

The choice of container needs to complement the tulips grown. Wide-flowered tulips like low-growing Kaufmanniana Group tulips and double-flowered cultivars call for wide-topped containers. Tall-growing cultivars suit slim upright pots better. In either case, the colour of the pots and the materials they are made from need to be matched to their contents.

Many of the wild tulips grow well in pots and for the smaller-growing species this is the best way to appreciate them at close quarters. Often they may be left in their containers from one year to the next. Nothing could be simpler.

Containers filled with tulips can also play a useful role in a larger garden, bringing splashes of colour to areas that are filled with plants that peak at a later time in the year. Pots are also ideal for creating points of interest next to the front door of the house or framing an entrance. The advantage in every case is that once the display is over we can remove the pots or quickly replant them with new material, unlike when tulips are grown in the open ground, when we need to leave their leaves to grow and feed up next year's bulb. My experience shows that, unlike the species tulips, container-grown garden cultivars rarely produce new bulbs large enough to flower the following year; these are best thrown away. Therefore there is no point continuing to feed and water them after flowering unless they are a rare variety that you wish to save.

Bedding

Mass bedding has been a popular way of using tulips ever since its inception in the mid-nineteenth century. The style is best suited to large open spaces and in particular public parks, squares and roadsides. Seeing tulips used in this way does not really help us imagine how best to use them in the confines of a domestic garden, but by considering this approach perhaps we can draw some helpful conclusions.

The uniform, strongly coloured cultivars so frequently encountered in our city streets have been developed to provide a spectacular burst of colour that draws attention to the changing seasons and often to the architectural settings in which they are used. The tulip as an individually beautiful flower is ignored, as it is the mass effect that is required. Darwinhybrid tulips, which with their huge box-shaped flowers are perhaps the least elegant of the tulip groups, are amongst the most effective in these situations. However, this should not mean we reject such cultivars for the home garden, but rather that we should use them there in a different way, as I will be explaining later. In a public setting, such displays have their place: they are cheap and easily maintained, guaranteed to succeed and can simply be swept away and replaced by summer bedding to maintain a continuous display in high-profile situations.

Too often, however, such displays fail to receive our appreciation; in spite of their vibrancy, they can easily become monotonous and no more than a conventional part of the urban background. What is called for is a little more creativity and sensitivity, both in the selection of cultivars and in the ways they are arranged and associated with one another as well as with other possible companion plants. In Victorian Britain, park bedding was brought to perfection in spring, with tulips being arranged in grand formal schemes in combinations with hyacinths, daffodils and wallflowers and edged with biennials such as forget-me-nots, arabis, bellis and viola. Today, we encounter displays that aspire to the same aesthetic model but use a simplified planting palette – partly for economic reasons – that creates a diluted image

The Darwinhybrid 'Golden Parade' in a city square, Amsterdam

'Oranje Nassau' and 'Cardinal Mindszenty' (Double Early)

Informal style

'Couleur Cardinal' underplanted with *Festuca glauca* at Schiphol Airport, Amsterdam (Triumph)

costs of planting, maintaining and subsequently removing them.

The scale of the Schiphol scheme may not relate to conventional garden situations, but there could be occasions when the idea of using pots of tulips in a repeating grid pattern would work. A small courtyard, for example, that gives access to the buildings surrounding it, and is more often seen from within or above, could certainly benefit from the idea. Further, what Schiphol shows is that repetition of a strong element can have an impact far greater than the sum of its parts.

Conventional park bedding schemes using bulbs and hardy biennials have the drawbacks that they must be set out in autumn, have little impact throughout the winter and offer only three or four weeks of splendour in spring. One approach that overcomes some of these drawbacks is to use ground-covering perennials in place of the ephemeral biennials. The idea is to introduce something that has a longer season of interest, brings structure to the planting during the winter and is cheaper to maintain. Unfortunately, many of the plants selected for this job prove to be dreary alternatives to the exciting biennials they replace. Ivies, pulmonarias, periwinkles and geraniums are good ground covers for the garden, but they are all low growing and spreading. Their impact in winter varies and can often be effective, but even when they add flower colour to the bedding display their lack of stature is never dramatic and invariably the maintenance costs associated with them are higher than might at first be expected. Not only do these types of perennials spread beyond their allotted boundaries, but most need to be replanted every three years in order to maintain their vigour and attractiveness.

What is called for is a more adventurous selection of hardy perennials that bring diversity to these planting schemes and also introduce height and structure. Clearly this is easier said than done, for the plants must not only offer early spring interest but also be capable of surviving the rough and tumble of a public situation as well as offering their own effective seasonal display, be that flowers or foliage.

of what was once so lovingly executed. A hundred years down the road it is really time that those responsible for designing and planting our public spaces came up with some new contemporary ideas of their own. Budget constraints often mean that the Victorian approach fails, but there are alternatives that could offer the same visual impact and win public appreciation for far less expenditure.

Visit Schiphol Airport in Amsterdam in spring and you will be confronted by a dramatic display of Holland's most famous export product. Some thirty huge concrete pots, each filled with fifty scarlet red tulips, are arranged in a wide grid pattern in front of the main entrance. Nothing could be simpler; nor need it be more intricate, as this is a place where people are on the move: rushing to catch a plane, find their car or take a taxi, travellers will see the display in passing. Were this a place to sit and wait, the repetition and scale of the planting would quickly become boring, but here it doesn't. What is worth noting is that a vast space has been effectively filled with colour with relatively few plants. The Victorian approach would have called for a mass planting of ten times the number of bulbs and the associated

The Darwinhybrid tulip 'Gudoshnik' growing amongst perennials in my garden. The grasses include low, green *Sesleria autumnalis* and variegated *Calamagrostis* x *acutiflora* 'Overdam' in the background. A mound of *Aruncus diocius* is emerging in the foreground, while forget-me-nots, pulmonarias and *Scilla siberica* introduce blue tints and white-flowered sweet rocket (*Hesperis matronalis* var. *albiflora*) adds height and contrast.

Daylilies (*Hemerocallis* cultivars) are the first group of such plants that spring to my mind. These true perennials die down in autumn, but by early spring they have started back into growth and by the time the first of the tulips are coming into flower their fresh iris-like foliage is forming substantial clumps some 12 inches/30 centimetres tall. Cultivars vary in the time they appear and their rate of growth, which itself could bring variety to the planting scheme, but perhaps more interestingly, most have fresh green foliage while others bear leaves coloured chartreuse to almost bright yellow, particularly when first emerging. Daylilies flower for a long period in summer and are generally accepted as good tough perennials for public situations, and thus seem to fulfil our requirements perfectly.

Euphorbias are also perfect partners for tulips. Some are evergreen like the low-growing *E. amygdaloides* var. *robbiae*, but a particular favourite of mine is the deciduous *E. palustris*, which quickly rises to 39 inches/1 metre tall by the time the tulip season is at its peak. The one thing all euphorbias have in common is that although their tiny flowers come and go, these are surrounded by large, brightly coloured modified leaves called cyathium leaves.

These can remain effective for weeks if not months, as even when they fade their russet tints can make a valuable contribution to a summer planting scheme.

Grasses are another obvious option. Evergreen tufts of *Festuca glauca* can bring blue grey patterns to a bedding scheme throughout the year, but share the weakness of more conventional choices by being ground-level players. Tall-growing deciduous cold-season grasses offer more potential as these leap into growth the moment temperatures pull away from freezing in the spring. I cannot have enough of *Calamagrostis* x *acutiflora* for its stiff upright architectural qualities throughout summer, autumn and winter. In spring its fresh green foliage grows extremely fast and by mid-spring it is making bold clumps over 20 inches/50 centimetres tall. The leaves are fine and spiky, bringing a zingy contrast to the more solid-looking tulip flower heads that make its perfect partner at this time of the year. For the public situation, as indeed for the home gardener, the bonus of cold-season grasses is that they do their growing in the early part of the year, reach flowering maturity early and then slip into dormancy in high summer when

The coloured bark of *Cornus alba* 'Sibirica' with the Double Late tulip 'Red Princess'

within its design. Even more dramatic and also better suited to this technique are various species of willow (*Salix*) and dogwood (*Cornus*) and their many cultivars. What is so exciting about this idea is that these plants display a wide range of different-coloured stems throughout the winter which could be used to harmonize or contrast with a spring display of tulips. These range in colour from the black of *Salix gracilistyla* 'Melanostachys' and *S. myrsinifolia* (syn. *S. nigricans*) through various shades of yellow, green, the amber-barked cultivars of *S. alba* to the brilliant reds of *S.a.* 'Britzensis' and 'Cardinalis' as well as *Cornus alba* 'Sibirica', and the bright yellow of *C. sericea* 'Flaviramea' and the orange of *Salix* x *rubens* 'Basfordiana'. All these will erupt into life at the same time as the tulip's flowering, adding foliage tints from fresh green through to the rich red of *Prunus* x *cistena*. In the case of the willows, catkins, in shades ranging from red and yellow to white can extend the season of interest. Even cut stems of these shrubs inserted into the ground in autumn will root and shoot into growth the following spring, which could be an easy means of incorporating their colourful structure into a conventional bedding scheme.

temperatures rise. They do not therefore need irrigation, as do more conventional planting schemes and especially summer bedding plants.

By using tough clump-forming perennials and adopting modern mulching techniques, you can keep maintenance of these elements of bedding schemes to little more than an annual tidy-up and the reduction of the size of their clumps every three or four years.

Shrubs might also be incorporated in new approaches to bedding. Evergreens for backgrounds and topiary forms are nothing new, but I have in mind deciduous species that offer winter or spring interest and easy management. Coppicing is a technique that can offer great possibilities, as many shrubs respond well to the annual removal of their branches. The cutting back keeps the plants to a moderate size and is simple to carry out.

Various species of *Prunus*, if cut back hard after flowering, will grow back to reflower the following spring at the same time as their border companions. The dark stems of species such as *P. tenella* and *P.* x *cistena* could bring some structure to an area of bedding if they were arranged in bold simple blocks or lines

Tulips in garden borders

Bedding is an intensive form of gardening and even when a proportion of the ground area covered is allocated to hardy perennials, as proposed above, the time, effort and costs associated with it are high. Within the confines of small private gardens, the approach has limited appeal, as the priority is to maximize the available space to create a pleasing image throughout the year. The mixed border, where all conceivable types of plant are brought together to provide structure and year-round interest, has evolved to fulfil this need. A conventional flower bed would need to be repeatedly replanted with bulbs, early- and then late-flowering annuals to maintain a similar continuous display, with new plants being grown in a reserve area of the garden awaiting their turn in an endless cycle. In Victorian times labour and space were available to make this feasible, but rarely is that the case today. For fun, a gardener may set aside a small area for this type of display but is unlikely to adopt the approach throughout the whole garden. Tastes have changed as well as the size of our gardens, and nowadays tulips are more than likely to be used as integral parts of mixed planting schemes with trees and shrubs as their backgrounds and perennials, biennials and other bulbs as their springtime companions.

Cramming tulips together in mass bedding schemes robs them of their individuality. In contrast, when freed to emerge in discrete clumps or drifts throughout garden borders they regain their inherent grace and character. Subtle associations can be developed between their individual flower shapes and their varied flower colours, and the plants that surround them. Even cultivars that are conventionally thought of as typical bedding varieties like the Darwinhybrid 'Apeldoorn' or the Triumph 'Negrita' become exciting components of sophisticated schemes when their specific characteristics such as height and petal colour

LEFT Topiary and tulips

TOP RIGHT 'Black Parrot', 'Spring Green' (Viridiflora) and bluebells

BOTTOM RIGHT 'Doll's Minuet' (Viridiflora)

TOP LEFT 'Red Shine' (Viridiflora) and *Narcissus* 'Pipit'

TOP RIGHT Orange tulips and pale yellow daffodils flood this garden in mid-spring

BOTTOM 'Menton' (Single Late)

are selected to precisely match or even contrast with their neighbours.

Tulips never recline in the background; they are the stars not the chorus of our garden compositions. Wherever we use them they will stand out, drawing attention to themselves and the locations they are used in. As focal points, they can function in our gardens like any other, leading the eye and one's feet from place to place to reveal the design ideas we may be playing with. And as with conventional public bedding displays, they may be used to bring a particular part of the garden alive in celebration of the arrival of spring. The crucial point to grasp is that tulips are potent design tools and whenever we decide to use them we will need to plan carefully. All too often, the spontaneous purchase of a bag of bulbs in autumn results in a self-conscious clump of colour dropped randomly into the garden, drawing attention to its inappropriate placement, redeemed only by the fact that it is, after all, a jolly herald of spring.

There are two routes to be followed when deploying tulips in the garden. We can either use them to create a dominant spring theme or alternatively we can add them to existing planting arrangements to complement and enhance the effect; the tulip as either the theme or the companion is the choice to be made.

It is surprising to me how rarely we see tulips used as a bold dominant theme in private gardens. This is due in part to their negative image engendered by uninspiring park bedding and in part from their reputation as bulbs that only grow well in the first year of planting and thereafter dwindle away to nothing. I have already discussed the park bedding problem and don't really feel it should get in the way of gardeners taking up tulips and exploiting their intrinsic qualities. As for the problem of many tulips not returning to flower in subsequent years, there are ways around it. Firstly, we need to choose the best cultivars for the garden and avoid those bred for forcing under cover for cut flowers, many of which are regularly offered to us for sale. Secondly, we need to understand their requirements for optimum growth and in some cases be prepared to lift the bulbs for summer storage above ground. And thirdly, focus our attention on wild species, some of the so-called Botanical tulips and those hybrids with exceptional vigour that sets them apart from the run-of-the-mill tulips and allows them to be left in the ground from year to year where many will not only survive but increase in

LEFT Single Late tulips with pink *Cercis siliquastrum* and wisteria in the background

RIGHT Tulips are used to emphasize this garden's layout: Lily-flowered 'Elegant Lady' in the foreground and further back the white Fosteriana 'Purissima'

number. I will discuss my experience in these matters in chapters on pages 66–147 which consider the various groups of garden tulips.

My first success with using tulips as a spring planting theme occurred when I hit upon the idea of incorporating a bright red tulip called 'Red Shine' into a large border I was making using tall ornamental grasses and colourful perennials such as heleniums, rudbeckias, asters and eupatoriums, all of which do not reach their peak until late in the summer. In spring this border was lush with foliage in various tints of green but, in all honesty, it was dull and drifted into the background. Red being the complementary colour of green meant that the hundred bulbs I generously spread across the width of my grass border brought it centre stage, giving it an earlier and truly dramatic second season of interest.

This approach is not bedding in the conventional sense, as the tulips were spread randomly and far apart, but they covered the whole area and, because of the strong colour contrast, they dominated the scene and thereby became its theme.

In the Netherlands tulips can begin to flower in the second half of March, that is early spring, and some may still be making their contribution in the middle of May, late spring. In the beginning the garden is quite bare and even low-growing species tulips such as *Tulipa humilis* can have an impact, but by the middle of their season and certainly later, hardy perennials are growing up rapidly and only the tallest tulip cultivars are capable of being seen from afar when our aim is to create an overall planting theme.

I tend to place the earliest-flowering tulips nearest to regularly used access paths. These are some of the species tulips and early Kaufmanniana Group tulips, all of which are best enjoyed at close quarters where the refined beauty of their flowers and especially their interiors can be appreciated. As the season progresses, bolder themes can be created further back in the garden landscape using taller-growing cultivars. My aim is twofold: I want to celebrate the arrival of spring throughout the whole garden and progressively entice visitors deeper into its recesses. I have allocated different areas different colour themes and not all of them reach their peak at the same time. By the careful selection of cultivars, I aim to keep the show going for as long as possible and delight in the many different forms of tulip worthy of a place in the garden.

The area of my garden adjacent to the main gate is dominated by white tulips throughout their season, beginning with the Single Early 'Diana' followed by the Triumph 'Pax' and eventually Lily-flowered 'White Triumphator'. For contrast, dark tulips such as dark maroon 'Jan Reus' and near black 'Queen of Night' are sprinkled amongst the whites, while concentrated clumps of intensely vivid magenta 'Doll's Minuet' and 'Burgundy Lace' introduce a late-season crescendo to the scheme. This section of the garden contains many other spring-flowering plants such as white and pale yellow daffodils, blue scillas, anemones and pulmonarias as well as various forms of hellebore, but these serve to provide the setting for the tulips rather than creating a theme in their own right.

The effect would be different if instead of spreading the tulips across the whole area, I confined them to discrete clumps amidst their companions. Such decisions about how we organize and distribute bulbs throughout a planting scheme will have a huge influence on the final result. A few clumps here and there will be pleasant, adding to the composition by giving it more emphasis and drawing us into its intimate detail. However, by spreading the bulbs generously across the canvas, we introduce a clear and dominant theme which is more expansive and tends to make the space feel larger by broadening horizons.

The scheme I have just described is fairly sophisticated and has taken a number of years to perfect, but away from the street in the centre of the main garden I have decided to be far more brash. By the middle of the tulip season, shrubs like yellow forsythia and shocking pink cherry (*Prunus*) are fighting in the background, spring is unravelling with all the energy it can muster and I feel the need to shout about it. A bed planted with sun-loving perennials for high summer is underplanted with one of the toughest and most persistent of garden tulips, the Darwinhybrid 'Gudoshnik'. It is typical of its group, with large square-based flowers atop thick, tall, sturdy stems. This cultivar is slightly more interesting than some of its clan as the pale

'White Triumphator', 'Queen of Night' and 'Doll's Minuet' with *Narcissus* 'Thalia' (Lily-flowered/ Single Late/Viridiflora)

yellow flowers are splashed and streaked in pink and orange with no two flowers being exactly alike. Some are almost pure yellow while others are flooded with fiery colour. For a bold contrast, I have used the violet purple Triumph tulip 'Negrita', but this time I have juxtaposed the two cultivars rather than mixing them, for no better reason than to offer an alternative image to other tulip themes present in the rest of the garden.

The types of plants I have used in this border for its summer display are not very evident this early in the year, and in order to give the tulip theme a setting I have planted the border with clumps of biennial forget-me-nots (*Myosotis*) and perennial *Doronicum orientale* 'Finesse'. This easy perennial can also be treated as a biennial and planted out into the border in autumn. It flowers freely in April and May with large, clear yellow daisy flowers that fit perfectly into the boisterous scheme I am attempting to create.

The display of 'Red Shine' tulips in my grass border takes place later in the far recesses of the garden, but at the same time another theme is being explored in a border nearer to the house and, in its way, it can help explain an alternative approach to using tulips: that is, as companion plants. Here the idea is allowed to play itself out

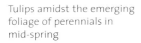

'Gudoshnik', a fine
Darwinhybrid tulip

Tulips amidst the emerging
foliage of perennials in
mid-spring

taking the theme forward. With their harsh yellow flower heads as the dominant colour theme, any tulips used here need to work with them rather than throwing up a counter argument. Yellow tulips in various shades and intensities were the obvious place to look and over the years I have tried different approaches. A wide drift of bright yellow Lily-flowered 'West Point' proved far too dominant and the Darwinhybrid 'Daydream', which opens pale yellow but quickly colours warm orange, also proved distracting. The answer came in the form of the Viridiflora Group tulip 'Spring Green', which has bowl-shaped creamy yellow flowers with the distinctive green stripe up the outside of each petal. Its colour dilutes and softens the harshness of the euphorbias while the green stripe picks up the delicate matrix of foliage textures that are the mainstay of this complex border.

When adding tulips into existing planting arrangements, we must pay great care and attention to every aspect of their character and habit. Once introduced, the tulip will take a leading role in any association and lead the eye towards the subtleties of form and colour of its companions. Large-flowered tulips such as all

across the whole area of this section of the garden, bridging the difference between the two different approaches.

The border explores an idea wherein various perennials succeed one another in a display that lasts from April until winter, with the scale and complexity of the composition rising steadily. Colour is evident in the border throughout. In early spring this is predominantly yellow, which becomes progressively toned down by white as summer approaches. Euphorbias are a major component, with different species sequentially

Darwinhybrids, many Single Late tulips and some Lily-flowered tulips may be out of scale in intimate compositions and are more likely to find their place in wider, thematic displays. The pointed reflexed petals of some Lily-flowered tulips harmonize with the sinuous foliage of grasses and irises, while the more rounded flowers of Single Early tulips work by introducing amorphous blobs of colour into more architectural backgrounds.

Scale and shape aside, it is the colour of tulips that leads our choices, but often there are complex gradations of tints and hues which can be emphasized when they are repeated in companion flowers or foliage. As always, detailed observations will be the key to any successful associations.

Repetition is fundamental to all good planting design both in order to emphasize the idea being expressed as well as to maintain simplicity and so avoid muddled, bitty results that simply lead to dilution and the loss of impact. We therefore have to consider how many different tulips to include in any planting scheme. Playing with early, mid-season and late varieties can work to keep a colour theme going over many weeks, but mixtures of tulips can very quickly result in a messy effect even when they are beautiful cultivars in their own right. Mixing tulips for different effects can be highly rewarding (see page 176) but care is essential: just think of those terrible mixtures of Early Double tulips regularly offered for sale in bulb catalogues.

'Daydream' and 'Spring Green', scattered randomly amongst the surrounding perennials (Darwinhybrid/ Viridiflora)

HOLLAND'S DISPLAY GARDENS

Think of Holland and the first things to come to mind are tulips, clogs, cheese and windmills. Tulips and other bulbous plants together with cut flowers have been making a significant contribution to the Dutch economy for over a hundred years and there seems to be no reason to think that this will change in the future. The marketing and promotion of bulbs has from the very beginning been given a high priority.

LEFT 'Parade' and 'Golden Parade' (Darwinhybrid)

BELOW Tulip blend ('Fiesta Gitano')

Keukenhof

Undoubtedly the best-known aspect of the association of Holland with bulbs is the yearly spring exhibition held at the Keukenhof garden in Lisse, South Holland, in the heart of the country's bulb-growing district near the coast. A visit to Holland in the spring must always include a visit to the Keukenhof and a drive around the bulb fields that surround it. The garden opened in 1949 to display the very best of what was being produced locally and today more than seven million bulbs are planted out each season in its rolling parkland landscape. It serves as a showcase for the industry and numerous flower exhibitions take place in its many greenhouses, bringing bulb exporters into contact with their trade clients while at the same time providing a major boost to Holland's tourist industry.

Garden snobs are heard to criticize the overwhelming displays of tulips and other bulbs bedded out under Keukenhof's ancient trees and around its enormous lake. However, they fail to take into account the garden's aims of being an exhibition space and public showcase; it is not a private garden. It offers gardeners the chance to see just about everything that is available, grown to perfection in a truly beautiful setting. And in my case, without the free access I have been given over many years, this book would never have been possible.

TOP Azaleas as a background to tulips

BOTTOM A busy day at Keukenhof

Dutch bulb fields

Hortus Bulborum

Less well known than Keukenhof, but equally important for the tulip enthusiast, is the collection of historic cultivars and species grown at the Hortus Bulborum in Limmen in North Holland. In a simple field behind the village church will be found row upon row of tulips, together with some daffodils, hyacinths, fritillaries and a few other bulbs. This is not a garden but a living collection of the oldest and most significant cultivars in the history of tulips. Here you can see the old Duc van Tol tulips, the Darwins that were used to breed today's Darwinhybrids, the breeders that gave rise to the broken flowers carefully groomed by the florists and a tangible glimpse of the flowers that once brought the Dutch economy to its knees.

The collection was begun by the local headmaster of the village school, Pieter Boschman, who in 1924 realized that many of the old cultivars were no longer grown in the region. It is thanks to him that today we have more than 2,500 cultivars to study. The Hortus Bulborum supplies historic gardens around the world with bulbs and serves as an important gene bank for the industry's breeding programmes.

TOP LEFT Breeder tulips such as 'Wilberforce' (front) and 'Winnetou' are no longer commercially available.

TOP RIGHT 'Zomerschoon' – raiser unknown, but grown since 1620 (Single Late)

BOTTOM LEFT This fine old Lily-flowered tulip, 'Mrs Moon', arose in Ireland around 1890.

BOTTOM RIGHT Hortus Bulborum, Limmen, the Netherlands

SPRING GARDENS AND TULIP COMPANIONS

Rarely will a garden be designed to provide a setting for tulips, but rather it will already exist and offer the opportunity for them to be incorporated into its design. Trees, shrubs, hedges and built structures will determine its framework and these together with the rest of its planting will, in varying degrees, influence which tulips to plant and how they might be used.

In early spring plants that are dormant will be less important than those that burst early into growth and draw attention through their flower colour or foliage. How best these can be associated with tulips will be influenced by both their scale and the moment they become effective.

Trees and shrubs

For a planting of tulips to establish a relationship with a tree you will have to use them in wide drifts or massed bedding schemes. In spring the most likely candidates for these associations will be the many species and cultivars of *Prunus*, which include the flowering cherries, almonds and apricots, of the ornamental crab apples (*Malus*) and of *Magnolia*. The predominant colour in all these is pink in varying intensities, with the addition of some pure whites and a few purple-tinted magnolias. With dramatic neighbours on such a scale, the tulip has no alternative but to play a supporting role, and any cultivars you choose will need to harmonize with their blossom. The suburban favourite, bright pink *Prunus* 'Kanzan', could be underplanted with the equally bold two-tone pink Triumph 'Gander's Rhapsody' for sheer drama; a more sophis-ticated approach might be to use a paler hue, as provided by the violet pink Triumph 'Lydia' or the very pale Single Early tulip 'Christmas Dream'. Prettier, paler-flowered cherries such as *Prunus* x *yedoensis* with its arching branches that bring their blossom nearer to the ground call for equally delicate pink partners or, alternatively, a darker contrast, as might be provided by a drift of the white-edged, deep purple violet Triumph tulip aptly named 'Arabian Mystery'.

White-flowered trees such as *Amelanchier lamarckii* with its fleeting spring display or magnificent cherries like *Prunus* 'Shirotae' (syn. 'Mount Fuji') and 'Taihaku' leave the field open for potential colour partners. Wide drifts of tulips in any colour will work and – in the absence of sugary pinks – yellow daffodils could be used with equally dramatic effect.

LEFT 'Queen of Night' (Single Late)

RIGHT Mid season in the Keukenhof garden, with Fosteriana tulips ('Candela'?) filling the foreground

ABOVE 'Stargazer'
(Triumph)

RIGHT
TOP *Corylopsis*
MIDDLE *Forsythia*
BOTTOM *Prunus*

Shrubs are more in scale with tulips than trees and can offer a colourful setting in which to place them. I have already mentioned the colourful barks of many *Salix* and *Cornus* species as potential companions (see page 34). These vigorous shrubs make excellent background plants during the summer months, especially those with the added bonus of colourful or variegated foliage, but their vibrant winter stems are their most important feature.

Flowering shrubs are few at the beginning of the tulip season, making those that there are all the more precious. *Daphne mezereum* wreathes its bare branches with hard pink flowers between February and April. At less than 39 inches/ 1 metre tall, it is a typical plant of the cottage garden and perfectly in scale with any of the early-flowering tulips. I can imagine surrounding its ankles with diminutive *Tulipa humilis* as early as the middle of March; the combination of violet purple and pink would be thrilling. But just think how psychedelic it could become some two weeks later if you were to include carrot orange *T. praestans* 'Fusilier' in this grouping.

The daphne's colour could be contrasted with the white Single Early tulip 'Diana' or alternatively, if you grew the white form *Daphne mezereum* f. *alba*, the colours could be swapped over and you could surround it with cherry pink Single Early 'Christmas Marvel' or one of the earlier-flowering Kaufmanniana tulips such as petite, pink 'Heart's Delight'.

Another early white-flowering shrub that would work in similar combinations is *Spiraea thunbergii*. This small irregular, rounded shrub clothes itself in tiny pale green leaves before the flowers appear in early spring. Its soft tints could not fight with anything, but it looks fresh and harmonious with light yellows such as the Single Early 'Bellona' or surrounded by drifts of Kaufmannianas such as the white with yellow base 'Franz Léhar', pale yellow 'Johann Strauss' or the darker yellow with red 'Giuseppe Verdi'.

Of the many types of *Prunus*, both trees and shrubs, the one I would not be without, and have deliberately added to my front garden's tulip scheme, is *P. tenella*. This small (5 feet/1.5 metres)

'Maureen' with *Exochorda* x
macrantha 'The Bride'
(Single Late)

upright shrub covers its bare branches with many delicate single pink flowers in the middle of the tulip season. Pink, purple and white tulips are its perfect companions and in my garden it nestles between Fringed 'Blue Heron' and white Triumph 'Pax', and at its feet a scattering of bright blue *Scilla siberica* completes the picture. *Prunus cerasifera* 'Rosea' (syn. *P. spinosa* 'Rosea'), a double pink hybrid between *P. cerasifera* 'Nigra' and the common hedgerow sloe *P. spinosa*, is comparable, a little later flowering with the added bonus of rich maroon purple foliage that is just starting to break open at the time of flowering. Another shrub in this same group, which I have yet to find and grow, is *P.* 'Rosea', the double pink hybrid of the common hedgerow sloe. Much smaller than the wild species, but equally spiny, it flowers while still devoid of its leaves in early April.

Small-scale shrubs such as those mentioned above lend themselves to mixing with their companions in an informal cottage garden style, but larger-growing shrubs are more likely to be placed to fill in the background. These are the common shrubs of springtime: brassy yellow forsythia, hard yellow kerria and the shocking pink-flowering currant *Ribes sanguineum*. These cheap and cheerful shrubs are rarely used well and all too often juxtaposed in clashing colour combinations. Wherever they occur you should take steps to integrate them into the picture as they all stand out sharply in the open spring landscape. Yellow forsythia and kerria call for drifts of yellow and white daffodils and tulips at their feet while the ribes must be kept away from all this yellow and moulded into its own candyfloss concoction. I would think of using Single Early tulips such as cherry pink 'Christmas Marvel' and paler 'Christmas Dream' mixed together with the contrasting flower shapes of the bright pink Double Early tulip 'Peach Blossom'. With the foreground filled with drifts of small-flowered *Chionodoxa luciliae* 'Pink Giant', the common flowering currant could become the star of the moment.

When designing a garden don't shun these shrubs, as they are full of the exuberance that typifies springtime. Each can be obtained in forms that are more desirable than those typically encountered. *Forsythia* x *intermedia* 'Lynwood Variety' has larger flowers than the common form; for me, the paler yellow 'Spring

Carex elata 'Aurea' with orange 'Daydream', yellow 'Mrs John T. Scheepers' and creamy 'Spring Green' (Darwinhybrid/ Single Late/Viridiflora)

Glory' is better still. *Kerria japonica* is available in the double-flowered form 'Pleniflora' and the charming low-growing form with white-edged leaves, 'Variegata'. However, my preference is for 'Golden Guinea', which has larger, deeper yellow single flowers. *Ribes sanguineum* comes in many shades of pink and red, but the one I grow is pure sophistication with its gleaming white flowers; its name 'White Icicle' seems to fit it perfectly.

For a taller pink-flowered shrub in this season, my vote goes to *Staphylea holocarpa* 'Rosea', which can become quite tall and gangly with age. The flowers are borne in clusters amidst the unfurling pinnate foliage, opening bright light pink from darker pink buds.

If there were one spring-flowering shrub I would encourage people to plant to augment their tulip display, it would have to be *Corylopsis spicata*. As a genus, corylopsis are shrubs for open woodland with moist acid soil. *C. pauciflora* is most commonly encountered, its primrose yellow flowers generously spread across its twiggy skeleton in early spring. In contrast, *C. spicata* is far less refined; its branches are held stiffly upright, but its advantages are that the flowers are larger and a brighter shade of yellow, affording them greater impact over distance; it is strongly scented and, equally importantly, it will grow in any moist fertile soil

without demanding acid conditions. In a way, this makes a sophisticated alternative to forsythia and calls for similar planting partners. One combination I saw that I particularly admired included the Fosteriana tulip 'Orange Emperor' and the tall white narcissus with an orange trumpet, 'Professor Einstein', with a corylopsis in the background.

Acid soils and woodland conditions are far from the natural home of the tulip, which is why I would not think of associating rhododendrons and azaleas with tulips. However, they both flower in spring and will, in certain gardens, be seen together. With colourful shrubs such as these filling the background, you will have to choose tulips that coordinate with them in some way. The only tulip that will actually thrive amongst these woodlanders is *T. sprengeri*. This extraordinary species is the very last tulip to flower, usually in late May in the Netherlands. Its bright scarlet red flowers will place clear limits on the colours that can be used near by; for example, pinks would look terrible.

Towards the end of the tulip season many more of the shrubs we associate with early summer start to flower. The list is long and includes the ubiquitous ceanothus, cercis, clematis, deutzias, lilacs, wisteria and weigelas. By this time Single Late, Lily-flowered and Viridiflora tulips are at their peak, and these offer endless possibilities for developing harmonious and contrasting colour themes. Additionally, deciduous beech and hornbeam hedges become clothed in fresh gleaming foliage that will increase the feeling of enclosure in the garden. Now the role of the tulip changes from one capable of creating wide drifts of colour in the open garden landscape to that of an accent plant in separate, intimate, jewel-like compositions.

Early spring partners

Within the garden's framework many perennials, bulbs and sometimes biennials are available to share the stage with tulips. At the beginning of early spring their numbers are few, but by late spring the tulips have to struggle above them for our attention. Fortunately, many of the low-growing tulip species and their cultivars flower early and avoid being overshadowed by their neighbours. *T. humilis* in shades of pink and purple and carrot coloured *T. praestans* are amongst the first to make a significant contribution in my own garden, and these find amiable company in the form of starry-flowered *Anemone blanda*, dark blue *Scilla bifolia* and the first few blooms on ground-covering perennials such as pulmonarias, *Brunnera macrophylla* and *Trachystemon orientalis*.

During these earliest days of spring, planting schemes can tend to lack structure and an adequate background, unless of course this is provided by a wall, fence or evergreen foliage. Therefore, at ground level, any plants that can offer sufficient bulk and form to introduce height, texture and pattern to our planting schemes will be indispensable. Clumps of *Helleborus* x *hybridus* will have been making their mark in many gardens for more than a month before the first tulips appear, but their flowers remain effective for many weeks. By early spring these are beginning to be joined by their freshly emerging handsome foliage, the old foliage having been cut away just prior to flowering, as good husbandry of these plants requires. At around 20 inches/50 centimetres tall, these clumps help break up the horizontal plan that can dominate our borders at this time and their flower colours can be coordinated with neighbouring flowers. Other species of hellebore such as *H. foetidus* and the more tender *H. argutifolius* can be even more effective as these have substantial evergreen foliage that creates a firm background in front of which flowering displays can readily be arranged.

Just as effective, *Arum italicum* subsp. *italicum* 'Marmoratum', with its dark green glossy foliage and silver tracery along the veins of its arrow-shaped leaves, has to be one of my all-time-favourite perennials. It dies down in summer to reawaken in autumn by throwing up green pencil-thick stems topped with clustered rows of bright red berries. While these are fun, the foliage, which emerges before Christmas, is sumptuous and remains pristine throughout the spring. White flowers are its perfect companions,

starting with snowdrops in late winter and then white tulips and daffodils, although any colour can be presented against the stylish background created by this easy perennial.

A setting for tulips can be made by many ground-covering plants including ivies, epimediums and carpet-forming perennials such as *Persicaria affinis*, which, although deciduous, retains its dry russet-tinted foliage through the winter. Many typical rock garden plants can also create evergreen carpets through which tulips might emerge. Some of the easiest and most robust are probably the best and could be used instead of the conventional biennials in more formal bedding displays. *Aubrieta* covers its mounds of evergreen foliage with colourful flowers just as the bulk of the bedding tulips reach their peak. With colours ranging from white through shades of violet, purple and blue to almost red the possible colour combinations it offers are many. *Iberis sempervirens* is just as common. The mounds of fine-textured foliage are dark glossy green, which contrasts sharply with the sheets of tiny pure white flowers that cover them in mid-spring. No white tulip will look as white as this, and therefore any other colour will make a better partner.

A less well-known carpeter that I find makes the perfect companion to some of the larger-growing species tulips such as *T. hageri*,

Blue flowers of pulmonaria, the bold foliage of ligularia and the fresh green blades of *Calamagrostis* x *acutiflora* 'Overdam'

Arum italicum subsp. *italicum* 'Marmoratum'

also the woodrushes (*Luzula* spp.) are evergreen and offer many possibilities for building the framework of a border display.

Euphorbias

Euphorbias are an extremely important group that offer many possibilities throughout the whole gardening year. One of the largest hardy species, *E. characias*, can develop into monumental clumps over 39 inches/1 metre high and wide that begin to flower in early spring and remain colourful until early summer. These are commonly referred to as subshrubs, meaning that they make a fairly permanent structure of stems, which in this case are clothed with evergreen whorls of grey-green pinnate leaves and bear bold yellow flowerheads at their tips. These are really plants for the background, but more useful, I find, are lower-growing species that can be used to edge planting schemes, as in the case of *E. amygdaloides* var. *robbiae,* or dotted randomly throughout them, as might be done with the compact mounds of *E. polychroma*. These both grow around 20 inches/50 centimetres tall and bear their bright chartreuse yellow flowerheads over many weeks in early spring. The deciduous species *E. palustris* is similar but grows taller and looser and is more suited to wilder schemes or for building drifts of background colour. In my own garden, I use all these euphorbias together to create a scheme with a common theme but subtle variations which is flooded later in the season with drifts of creamy yellow 'Spring Green' tulips which are succeeded by the tall drumsticks of the ornamental onion *Allium hollandicum* 'Purple Sensation'.

For the sake of completeness, we should not forget one more euphorbia for later combinations, *E. griffithii* 'Dixter'. The flower colour is terracotta red which becomes effective around the same time as the late-flowering tulips such as the scarce orange 'Dillenburg', multi-flowered 'Orange Bouquet', deep purple 'Recreado', pure red 'Halcro' and the Double Late maroon 'Uncle Tom', all of which could be used to build sumptuous schemes around it.

T. marjolletii (syn. *T. marjolettii*) and *T. whittallii* is *Arabis procurrens*. From low, mid-green mounds of fine-textured foliage its flowers rise to around 12 inches/30 centimetres, white, small and held in open clusters. The effect is airy, soft and gentle and when it is out of flower the evergreen foliage continues to looks neat and attractive.

The foliage of many perennials is just as important as the flowers they will eventually produce. We have seen how the emerging leaves of many *Hemerocallis* cultivars can be highly effective early in the year. Likewise, *Asphodeline lutea*, which flowers yellow in May along with the late-season tulips, has attractive grey green grass-like foliage throughout the winter months. This is more succulent in texture than any of the glaucous-leaved grasses that might also be considered in similar situations.

A number of ornamental grasses are attractive in early spring, such as the dense green mats of *Sesleria autumnalis* and the freshly emerging foliage of *Calamagrostis* x *acutiflora* (see page 33). In shady conditions, *Milium effusum* 'Aureum' is effective very early in the spring. It is bright yellow in all its parts, growing loosely and elegantly to reach 24 inches/60 centimetres tall by flowering time in early summer. A richer golden yellow can be provided by dense clumps of Bowles's golden sedge, *Carex elata* 'Aurea'. Other sedges and

Bulbous companions

Spring is far from being the exclusive preserve of the tulip. Many other bulbous plants take advantage of the early lack of shade from deciduous trees and the rise in temperatures to rush into bloom before retreating below ground. Snowdrops (*Galanthus* spp.) and bluebells (*Hyacinthoides non-scripta*) are classic examples from woodland habitats, while daffodils thrive in more open settings that later in the year become too hot for comfort. Within the varied aspects of our gardens, we usually succeed in bringing together plants from a range of different habitats, opening up many exciting possibilities for planting associations that would never occur in nature.

The snowdrops and winter aconites (*Eranthis hyemalis*) have finished by the time the tulips arrive, but other low-growing species are waiting to take their place. Many of these are blue-flowered and are perfect for planting in drifts between taller-growing neighbours including tulips. *Scilla bifolia*, just 4 inches/10 centimetres tall, may still be around when the first of the species tulips begin to flower, but the universally popular *S. siberica* takes over its strong blue mantle and stays effective for several weeks, in time to join the bulk of the early and mid-season tulips. The cultivar 'Spring Beauty' grows 6 inches/15 centimetres tall; it is darker blue than the wild species, but more expensive, which might be important if you are planting large quantities.

The so-called glory of the snow rarely lives up to its name in my garden, coming into flower in early spring along with *Tulipa praestans* and the Kaufmanniana tulips. It is listed as *Chionodoxa luciliae* in bulb catalogues but its correct name is *C. forbesii*. Each flower stem, some 8 inches/ 20 centimetres tall, carries up to ten clear blue flowers with a prominent white centre. There are several cultivars, including 'Blue Giant', all white 'Alba', pale-tinted 'Pink Giant' and 'Rosea'. They need to be planted in quantity to have an impact and fortunately the clumps increase in size each year as well as producing seed that also aids their spread. Shorter-growing (6 inches/15 centimetres tall) *C. sardensis* makes a change from the common forms. It is a deeper blue than *C. luciliae* with only a very small white eye at the centre of each bloom and is renowned for freely setting seed.

There is a charming, stocky, naturally occurring hybrid between *C. luciliae* and *Scilla bifolia* with deep blue flowers called x *Chionoscilla allenii*. Worthy of a place in the

garden, this is something to acquire if you are offered bulbs; or possibly you could attempt to grow your own by planting its parents together and following the progress of their seedlings.

Another common early blue is *Puschkinia scilloides*. Equally short and slightly later flowering than the others, it needs plenty of sunshine to perform at its best. Up to six flowers are clustered together on their short flowering stem which, in my opinion, gives them a rather bunched-up graceless form when compared with the others, but they are easy and useful for bringing variety to the garden.

Grape hyacinths (*Muscari*) are the quintessential blue flowers of spring, but they are commonly criticized for their untidy foliage. When it appears in autumn it is quite fresh and attractive; it makes an acceptable background for the flowers in spring, but keeps growing for weeks after their display is over, eventually turning yellow and dying. This unsightly problem arises when the bulbs are planted along the edges of paths and borders, but if the bulbs are scattered around within a mixed border planting the old leaves simply disappear behind the emerging foliage of their neighbours.

Muscari armeniacum is most commonly grown, but there are cultivars which flower for longer and offer variations in colour. 'Blue Spike' has double flowers with consequently more impact; it is 10 inches/25 centimetres tall, flowers for a long time and is heavily scented. 'Cantab' is shorter and later flowering, with bright Cambridge blue flowers that look perfect in combination with the pale pink Double Late tulip 'Angélique' as does *M.a.* 'Saffier', which has ball-shaped flowers rather than the typical tubes, in an exquisite shade of sapphire blue.

There are many other species of *Muscari*, some of which flower too late for our purposes or require specialized growing conditions. This is not the case with *M. azureum*, 6 inches/15 centimetres tall, which self-sows freely to create wide patches of bright blue in early spring. *M. aucheri* is slower to multiply, but no more difficult to grow. It has two-tone flowers: pale blue infertile flowers above and cobalt blue fertile ones below, atop flower stems just

4 inches/10 centimetres tall. However, the most useful when it comes to combinations with tulips is the taller-growing two-tone *M. latifolium*. As its name implies, it has one long broad leaf above which the flower stem rises some 10 inches/25 centimetres. Its flowers are bold and distinctive: lilac blue sterile flowers at their tips with dark indigo purple fertile flowers below. Its scale and rich colouring give it sufficient presence for it to be used in small groupings or widely scattered throughout a planting scheme rather than requiring to be mass planted for effect, as is the case with all the others.

We are now well into the tulip season when three bulbous plants arrive with sufficient stature to be used in balanced planting associations with the many mid- and late-season tulips jostling for attention in our borders. The first of these begins to flower in my garden at the beginning of April, but will still be making a valuable contribution one month later. The common name of summer snowflake for *Leucojum aestivum* seems quite wrong for a plant that flowers so early, but presumably it is used because it flowers after the spring snowflake (*L. vernum*), which blooms along with the snowdrops to which these similarly white-flowered plants are related. Do not grow anything other than the strong and vigorous form *L.a.* 'Gravetye Giant', which reaches 24 inches/60 centimetres tall when given moist fertile conditions. Clusters of white bells with charming green spots at the tip of each petal dangle from the top of the sturdy flower stems. Refined and elegant and yet imposing enough to hold their own against the company of elegant tulips, these white flowers are tulips' perfect accompaniment.

Crown imperials are the next imposing bulbous plants to enter the stage. These are one of the biggest members of a large genus of bulbs that belong mainly to woodland; however, *Fritillaria imperialis* is the exception, requiring full sun as well as rich soil in order to grow and thrive. They grow 32 inches/80 centimetres tall with clusters of large bell-shaped flowers near the top of sturdy stems which bear a tufted

rosette of leaves at their tips. Traditionally they are used in bedding schemes as accent plants rising out of the surrounding mass of tulips and biennials. It is almost impossible to find them grown without tulips in the vicinity, but I am not so sure that the two plants make the best partners. For once it seems the tulip has met its match and the two divas are engaged in a contest for supremacy. Instead, I suggest that these splendid flowers are used in place of and away from tulips, possibly in alternating schemes where each is allotted the leading role. Within a colour-themed border they make a perfect accent plant and, when grouped together, a strong focal point. The colour range is however fairly limited to just yellow and various shades of orange red, with some forms having white- or yellow-variegated leaves.

Our third statuesque bulbous partner arrives at the end of the tulip season. *Camassia leichtlinii* subsp. *suksdorfii* Caerulea Group is the first of three species in this genus to make an important contribution to gardens. They grow best in moist soil conditions and so you need to find a point of compromise between their needs and those of tulips (see page 183). From tufts of lax iris-like foliage, stiffly erect stems ascend some 27 inches/70 centimetres and are covered for more than half of their length with violet blue

ABOVE The green tips of *Leucojum aestivum* 'Gravetye Giant' in harmonious association with the Viridiflora tulip 'Spring Green'

OPPOSITE
TOP The Greigii tulip 'Orange Elite' and *Narcissus* 'Bridal Crown', next to a river of *Muscari armeniacum*

BOTTOM *Muscari latifolium*

Camassia leichtlinii subsp. *suksdorfii* Caerulea Group brings height and contrast to a scheme with the Lily-flowered tulip 'Ballade' in the background and the Triumph 'Don Quichotte' and *Geranium tuberosum* filling in the foreground.

star-shaped flowers. Their slim elegant form contrasts with the rounder, denser shapes of tulip flowers and should ideally be intermingled with them. Their colour is unusual, as if grey slate has been used in mixing the tint, a suggestion of which is also to be found in the pink of the strangely crumpled flowers of the Single Late tulip 'Picture'. Put the two together for a truly sophisticated contrast and if you were to add the violet pink cocktail-sausage flowerheads of *Persicaria bistorta* 'Superba' and the fluffy off-white pompoms of the snowy woodrush (*Luzula nivea*), the scheme would have sufficient presence to fill an entire border.

Camassia cusickii has broader flower spikes with the most exquisite ice blue flowers. Some years it will flower early enough to catch the last of the tulips and when it does the effect can be magical. *C. leichtlinii* 'Alba' flowers later again; it is slightly taller, but regrettably only a plant to follow on from the tulips and not one to associate with them. This is also true of the

ornamental onions, *Allium hollandicum* and its selection 'Purple Sensation'; most years they flower early and join the last of the tulips, but it is not an association that you can ever depend upon.

No garden can afford to be without daffodils in spring and there are species and numerous cultivars in flower from the last days of winter all the way through until early summer. Whole books have been written about them and I, like most keen gardeners, never fail to find something to bring home when visiting a collection of these bulbs. I have already explained that I feel these are plants for massing into drifts for filling in the background and creating sheets of seasonal colour. When they are grown alongside tulips they must always play a supporting role by either forming a background or, when mixed together, by never attempting to dominate through their greater size or brighter colours. The big bold daffodils that tempt us in bulb catalogues are better suited to the exhibition table or vase and rarely look appropriate in the open spring garden. Rather than plunge into a detailed description of daffodils I shall instead highlight the few I have grown which seem to enhance the garden in spring and more particularly combine well with my tulips.

The wild *Narcissus pseudonarcissus* flowers early, with pale yellow nodding flowers and a central trumpet of a slightly darker shade. At only 12 inches/30 centimetres tall, they mix perfectly with orange red *Tulipa praestans* 'Fusilier', with which they make a light contrast, but put them next to the rich yellow and red Kaufmanniana 'Stresa' and they look pale and uninteresting. These are informal characters that look best in a wild situation; I use them along the edges of a woodland path with pools of pale-tinted Kaufmanniana tulips set further back between the trees and shrubs.

Like most gardeners, I have Cyclamineus *Narcissus* 'February Gold' dotted around the garden. Some years it lives up to its name but mostly it flowers in March. I do not grow this to blend with tulips, but rather as a brightly coloured harbinger of spring; however, another Cyclamineus daffodil called *N.* 'Jack Snipe' flowers later and makes up a part of one of my planting schemes. This variety is shorter than most of its clan, some 8 inches/20 centimetres tall, with creamy white reflexed petals around a clear yellow cup. It naturalizes well and brings a freshness to a border in which dark blue pulmonarias flourish and provide a background to white-flowered tulips. Later in the season, the role of 'Jack Snipe' is taken over in the same border by the pure white Triandrus daffodil *N.* 'Thalia'. This grows to 15 inches/35 centimetres tall and each stem carries up to three flowers. The informal character of this daffodil suits it for use in such a mixed planting scheme in which the white tulips are eventually joined by dark maroon Triumph tulip 'Jan Reus' and still later dusky 'Queen of Night'; being white, *Narcissus* 'Thalia' mixes easily with everything around it.

I seem to have a preference for white daffodils as another I use alongside violet and purple

Triumph tulips later in the spring is one of the Small-cupped division called *N.* 'Polar Ice'. It grows about 18 inches/45 centimetres tall and its neat cup is faintly shaded green. Scale is so important and many of the large-cupped and trumpet daffodils are far too big for small to medium-sized gardens. Another of the Small-cupped types I use for background drifts of colour is *N.* 'Barrett Browning'. With broad white petals surrounding a small orange cup, the flowers have more substance than 'Polar Ice' but are still held only 18 inches/45 centimetres high. Unlike many similar light-toned older cultivars that they have essentially replaced in the assortment, their flowers look straight ahead as opposed to hanging their heads downwards.

The last daffodil to flower in my garden I have deliberately chosen to create a background to a display of toffee-coloured tulips: namely, Lily-flowered 'Ballerina', *T. acuminata* and *T. whittallii*. It is the multi-flowered Jonquilla daffodil *Narcissus* 'Pipit'. This variety is 15 inches/35 centimetres tall with relatively small flowers that are lemon yellow fading to pure white at the centre. They grow alongside bold clumps of dark-leaved *Ligularia dentata* 'Desdemona', which accentuates their clear bright colouration. The sturdy-growing creamy white *Narcissus* 'Pueblo' would make a good substitute and where a standard pure yellow would be more appropriate I would use yet another of the Jonquilla daffodils called *N.* 'Quail'. This is wonderful in pots as well as the garden, and only grows 10 inches/25 centimetres tall.

My final comment on spring bulbs may not meet with universal agreement, but make it I must. Just because plants flower at the same time does not automatically mean they should be used side by side. Large-flowered Dutch crocus have their uses, but every spring I see them used in bedding schemes as an understorey to tulips and I hate it. Admittedly the crocus come in a range of splendid colours and can make interesting contrasting or harmonious associations with the tulips, but their goblet-shaped flowers look heavy and vulgar in such close proximity to the far more elegant tulip flowers and the result is simply ugly. I have a

Narcissus 'Jack Snipe' and white-flowered *Pachyphragma macrophyllum* with *Pulmonaria* 'Blue Ensign' behind

similar problem with hyacinths. I can think of nothing more majestic than a mass bedding scheme of these expensive bulbs, and anyone visiting the formal hyacinth garden at Anglesey Abbey, in Cambridgeshire, England, could not fail to be impressed. But hyacinth cultivars have a solid formality that is at odds with the sinuous elegance of tulips, in whose company they end up looking stiff and awkward. In this case, however, there is a way around the problem. In historical collections you will sometimes find examples of the wild *Hyacinthus orientalis* which was used in the early development of the current assortment of cultivars. These plants have far slighter, more open and, needless to say, less impressive flowerheads, but they look more natural and are far easier to combine with other plants including haughty tulips.

Perennial partners

Perennial plants, which include the bulbs, the ornamental grasses and the ground-covering plants I have already discussed, bring colour, texture and seasonal variety to our gardens. Some people demand low-maintenance gardens and shun perennials for being ephemeral and transient, but a garden filled just with evergreen shrubs and trees remains static all year, whereas the addition of perennials introduces a dynamic expressive element that I personally find essential.

Tulips are undeniably ephemeral. They flower for just a few weeks in spring and not all of them can be expected to repeat the performance the following year. It is this transience combined with their exquisite beauty and extravagant colours that makes them so appealing. However, a garden must function every day of the year and tulips can account for only a part of our plans. Bedding is one approach where they are quickly replaced once past their peak, but a more practical option in smaller gardens is to build a mixed scheme in which tulips make their contribution along with other types of plant. Perennials that flower bring colour into our garden pictures and invite associations, be these harmonious or contrasting, with the things that surround them.

Tulips, being primarily elements of colour, will likewise interact with their surroundings and offer endless possibilities for associating with nearby perennials.

Many of the perennials that flower in spring are low growing and often recommended for use as ground cover. They ideally clothe the soil's surface and create the setting for tulips. Pulmonarias are at the top of my list as they are at their peak of flowering from the moment the first of the Single Early tulips arrive and are still effective a month later when the late tulips are taking up the baton for the final stretch of the tulip season. *Pulmonaria* 'Blue Ensign' is my favourite, with dark green unmarked leaves with a rumpled, sculptural quality. The deep pure blue flowers are the largest of any pulmonaria, making this the best within this colour range. It grows 15 inches/35 centimetres tall, and with its absolute resistance to mildew in summer (which can be a problem with some of the better-known cultivars) it makes a good setting for any light-coloured tulips and daffodils. 'Blue Ensign' is one of many good blue cultivars; others to look for are 'Beth's Blue', 10 inches/25 centimetres tall, and 'Blauer Hügel', at 20 inches/50 centimetres tall one of the most impressive of all cultivars.

Red-flowered pulmonarias also have their uses. For years I grew *P. rubra* 'Redstart' with its coral red flowers underneath a bush of *Photinia* x *fraseri* 'Red Robin' which bore fresh new leaves in the same hue to stunning effect each spring. Had I then been aware of tulips I could have added one of the Fosteriana tulips such as 'Orange Emperor' or scarlet 'Madame Lefeber' for a show-stopping display. The leaves of this species are coarse pale green without any markings and make useful, unassuming ground cover. *Pulmonaria rubra* 'David Ward' (12 inches/30 centimetres) is a little more interesting with a wide white margin to the pale green leaves, but unfortunately these scorch easily and the plant needs to be carefully sited in light shade, making it less appropriate for use alongside tulips.

P. 'Sissinghurst White' (15 inches/35 centimetres) has pale green leaves spotted with silver white and pure white flowers. This is

probably still the best white, although *P. officinalis* 'White Wings' (10 inches/25 centimetres) is claimed to be more vigorous and floriferous and maybe that is correct. It died on me, but I now have my own seedling which appeared between the stepping stones next to the front gate; I call it 'Little White Gate'. It is very similar to 'Sissinghurst White', but the clumps are much more compact and rounded, and there is no susceptibility to mildew (yet). They are all indispensable and you should gather as many pulmonarias as you can find to create settings for spring-flowering bulbs, but you will need to go to a specialist nursery to find the best assortment.

Brunnera macrophylla starts to flower with the early tulips and is at its peak in their mid season. Its delicate blue flowers remind me of forget-me-nots held in loose flowerheads above the dark green, rough, rounded leaves. These can become coarse and ugly in the summer. To refresh their appearance it is advisable to cut the plants back completely after flowering, thereby encouraging fresh new foliage to spring up. The flowering period is not as long as the pulmonarias but by coinciding with them adds an extra dimension to a mixed planting. As well as the common blue-flowered species, there is a white-flowered cultivar called 'Betty Bowring' and a number of forms with attractively marked or variegated leaves. The best of these is 'Hadspen Cream', which has a broad cream to yellow band around the edge of the leaves. Unlike 'Dawson's White' (syn. 'Variegata'), which has white-margined leaves, it is far less susceptible to sun scorch.

White-flowered pulmonarias and brunnera help break up the predominance of blue that the bulk of their relatives bring to the garden along with the drifts of scillas, grape hyacinths and chionodoxas that may also be present, but there is another ground-cover plant that performs this task better than any. *Pachyphragma macrophyllum* flowers very early in the year, producing loose sprays of pure white flowers

A bed of *Calamagrostis* x *acutiflora* 'Overdam' edged with the fresh purple foliage of *Astilbe* x *arendsii* 'Fanal' becomes a dramatic focal point when furnished with the bold flowers of tall-growing Single Late tulip 'Big Smile'.

very similar to *Brunnera macrophylla,* in a display that continues for weeks on end. The flowers are set off against fairly large and rounded glossy leaves. Beth Chatto in *The Damp Garden* considers that these can make an attractive ground cover for the rest of the year, but with me they are not distinguished and seem to fade into the background. Perhaps if you grew wide patches of it her opinion would be validated. The plant is tough and will grow in dry shade, which is possibly why mine struggle a bit. Although the root is woody and difficult to divide, they are easily grown from seed and should be more frequently offered for sale than is currently the case.

Blue-flowered omphalodes begins to flower in the middle of the tulip season and remains effective through to the end. It makes subdued ground cover when out of flower with its comparatively smaller elliptical mid-green leaves, but makes a perennial alternative to billowing forget-me-nots in drier and shadier situations than these biennials would tolerate. There are two species: *O. verna* makes creeping rich green mats only 4 inches/10 centimetres high and is probably best suited to the wilder areas of the garden; *O. cappadocica* is the more refined plant, it spreads less vigorously, the leaves are more pointed and it grows 8 inches/20 centimetres tall. A larger-growing selection of *O. cappadocica* called 'Cherry Ingram' has darker gentian blue flowers than the type, but my

favourite is the clump-forming bright blue 'Starry Eyes', each of its flower's five petals boldly edged in white.

One excellent ground-covering perennial that should be grown in more gardens is *Trachystemon orientalis*. Its main attraction is its large heart-shaped leaves, mid-green and hairy, up to 12 inches/30 centimetres long and borne in ground-smothering mounds; as these emerge in spring, it throws up pretty starry blue flowers. Their effect is fleeting but, like any of the forget-me-not look-alikes, it can make delightful associations with early daffodils and tulips.

Another thug for clothing difficult corners and filling in the background, especially in the wilder parts of the garden, is symphytum. Looking through my notes on the garden in spring it is surprising how many times I have recorded its bold contribution. Like the *Trachystemon, Symphytum* is a member of the borage family with rough textured leaves, and there are a number of interesting species and cultivars to try if you have the space. My experience of them is limited, but the two that give me pleasure along with my mid-season tulips are 'Hidcote Blue' and 'Hidcote Pink'. Their leafy carpets are submerged by branching flower stems over 18 inches/45 centimetres tall, bearing clusters of tubular flowers, blue or orange pink at the base, fading to white at their tips.

As spring gets into its stride, the tough ground covers are joined by many other clump-forming perennials that begin to flower and offer themselves as partners for tulips. *Lamium maculatum* is a common low-growing ground cover that flowers with small magenta red or white flowers in spring. Far more interesting for our purposes is *L. orvula,* a neat, clump-forming species with dark, heavily veined leaves rising in compact rounded clumps some 20 inches/50 centimetres tall. The dark maroon flowers appear in whorls below the leaves at intervals up the length of each stem to create a smart solid form. It reaches its peak in mid season and continues through the time all the late-season tulips flower. Its dusky tones can be picked up with Triumph tulips such as dark red 'Bastogne', plum red 'Couleur Cardinal', crimson 'Jan Reus', brown red 'Cassini', dark pink 'Blenda' or, for pure theatre, 'Slim Whitman', which has dark brown red flowers with crisp golden yellow edges and dark green wavy leaves with golden yellow margins. Later contenders could include Single Late 'Black Horse', purple black 'Recreado', dusky pink 'Picture' or maybe some of the whites that are splashed and streaked in pinks and purples such as 'Shirley', 'Magier', 'Cordell Hull' or 'Montgomery'.

Pinks and purples abound with the arrival of the Triumph tulips in mid season and are well represented in the different classes of late-flowering tulips. Pink-flowering perennials are their obvious partners and these begin to arrive in abundance just at the right time. Foremost amongst them are the dicentras, with their locket-shaped flowers that dangle on gracefully arching stems above attractive fern-like foliage. The classic cottage garden bleeding heart is *D. spectabilis* with pink and white lockets spaced out along the arching stems up to 24 inches/60 centimetres tall. In truth, this is not a good companion for tulips as it needs moist, rich soil and light shade to thrive, but their association is a classic cliché that is probably worth the trouble of having to replace the bleeding heart every year. Slightly more robust and persistent, especially in more open

sunny situations, are forms of *D. eximia* and *D. formosa.* The leaves are more bluish grey and the plants more frothy than gracefully arching, but, nevertheless, they look well with light pink tulips. *D.* 'Luxuriant' did not cope with my heavy clay soil, which becomes hard and cracks in the summer. This was a pity as its rich cherry red flowers looked well with the Viridiflora tulip 'Esperanto'. Perhaps the slightly taller cultivar 'Adrian Bloom' or the dark pink 'Bountiful' would do better next time round.

Other classic cottage garden plants are in flower at the same time including Jacob's ladder (*Polemonium caeruleum*). This forms upright clumps of long stems lined with opposite pairs of pinnate leaves and 24 inch/60 centimetre tall branching stems of clear blue open bell-shaped flowers; these are lilac mauve in the case of 'Lambrook Mauve', the best selection.

The Triumph tulip 'Arabian Mystery' with *Lathyrus vernus* 'Alboroseus' as foreground

Veronica gentianoides

Solomon's seal (*Polygonatum* × *hybridum*) and various other *Polygonatum* species and cultivars are really plants of shady woodland, but like dicentras with arching, flower-strewn branches, which in this case bear milk white pearl-shaped bells, they make glorious associations with sinuous, upright tulips. Aquilegia, another woodlander, crops up wherever we fail to remove its seedlings, and it regularly mixes itself amongst my tulips. Where the colours work I allow them to stay; if not, they are easily removed. A small double form with dark purple flowers has arrived from somewhere and this one I encourage as it fits in everywhere and attracts a lot of admirers.

We should really look for true sun lovers as permanent tulip partners and one of the boldest is *Doronicum orientale*. These are bright yellow daisies that seem to have the same cheeky attitude to life as some of the brashest tulips, in particular the Darwinhybrids. There are many other species and hybrids which in the main flower a little later and can be invasive. This species makes neat clumps of light green rounded leaves that remain fresh all winter. The flowers appear in the middle of April in my garden and it grows some 20–24 inches/50–60 centimetres high.

Although this is a perennial plant that could be left where it is, it is also a plant that can be treated like a biennial and grown from seed each year. Spring-sown seedlings can be grown on in a spare plot during the summer and then set out in the autumn, either within a bedding scheme or wherever appropriate in the flower borders. The advantage of *D. orientale* is that it can be used in quantity for the spring show and then removed to leave space for the permanent members of the border for the rest of the year.

Thermopsis villosa (syn. *T. caroliniana*) is also yellow, but this time slightly lighter in tone, and the flowers are held on upright stems resembling delicate lupins. Other species in this genus are notorious for spreading out of control in the garden, and when I first grew this plant, I was determined to keep it under control. It too spreads, but I have discovered that it is not invasive; its slim stems and light foliage are quite

harmless, and wherever it appears in the border it looks delightful. It roams randomly through the euphorbias I grow in association with yellow, white and cream tulips, adding to the mix of tints and forms.

My latest discovery has been *Veronica gentianoides*. It comes into flower with the late-flowering tulips around the end of April here in the Netherlands. Spires of loosely borne pale blue flowers dance some 20 inches/50 centimetres above slowly spreading mats of broad dark green leaves. There are selections with pure white flowers and others tinted a stronger blue. As sun-loving plants, they enjoy the same conditions that will encourage tulips to perennialize (see page 181). Their delicate flowers work well with some of the taller late-flowering species tulips such as *T. acuminata*, *T. grengiolensis* – unfortunately a rarely available jewel – and *T. marjolletii,* and also with the shorter-growing Viridiflora tulips such as 'Golden Artist' and phlox pink 'China Town'.

Biennials in the spring garden

A true biennial is a plant that takes two growing seasons to reach maturity. Its seed germinates in the first year, seedlings overwinter and then come into flower the following year, whereupon they set seed and die. There are, however, some other true perennial plants that we can treat as biennials as they are capable of flowering well in their first spring. We have already seen the advantage of this approach when we met *Doronicum orientale* and another I use in this way is fennel (*Foeniculum vulgare*), which I grow for its feathery early-spring foliage.

The most popular biennial is forget-me-not (*Myosotis*). The foam of tiny flowers, blue or pink or white, it produces in late spring makes the perfect backcloth for displays of flowering bulbs and perennials. Once you have it, you always will, as forget-me-nots seed about freely; however, ideally, you should sow the seeds in early summer and line out the plants in a spare plot of land until autumn, when you can move them to where they are needed the following

spring. This is the method to follow with all biennials, as although many are offered for sale in garden centres, if you rely on buying them there you will not have any control over which cultivars and colours you might have available to use. In the case of forget-me-nots, for example, garden centres usually sell 'Blue Ball' or another compact variety that is ideal for use in pots and window boxes; but for the open garden we need taller more untidy varieties for weaving between the other plants in our borders.

Wallflowers (*Erysimum*) are the most exciting biennials for creating sumptuous displays in association with tulips. They are available in a range of heights and rich and exotic colours including maroons, chocolates and ambers or vibrant reds, lemons and yellows. To edge such displays, double-flowered daisies (*Bellis perennis*), vibrant-coloured polyanthus (*Primula* cvs.) and pansies (*Viola* x *wittrockiana*) are the traditional choices. Although one tends to think of bedding schemes when these plants are mentioned, there is nothing to stop us using them as temporary residents of the perennial borders in our gardens. Dotted informally amongst the emerging perennials, tulips and other seasonal performers, they can add considerably to the impact of a planting scheme.

For extra height, there are two indispensable and rather similar biennials, namely honesty and sweet rocket. Honesty (*Lunaria annua*) flowers from early to late spring. Its four-petalled flowers appearing in open branched flowerheads up to 36 inches/90centimetres high are usually intense purple, but can be found in shades of pink as well as the highly desirable white form. At all costs avoid the white variegated form, which looks brash and diseased. After seed has been formed, the pods shed their outer coverings to reveal translucent silvery discs that are commonly used in dried flower arrangements. Their scent comes as a bonus.

Sweet rocket (*Hesperis matronalis*) flowers slightly later, but usually early enough to join the Darwinhybrids and all the later-flowering tulips. The large billowing flowerheads are lilac, purple or white depending upon the strain grown and their scent is delicious and heavy, especially in the evening and at night. In truth this plant is perennial, but it flowers best in its first year and will normally die out when still fairly young. It seeds profusely and will, like honesty, always remain with you once introduced into the garden.

Other biennials, including Canterbury bells (*Campanula medium*), Brompton stocks (*Matthiola* cvs.), sweet Williams (*Dianthus barbatus*) and foxgloves (*Digitalis purpurea*), follow on to maintain interest in the borders in the early days of summer, but by the time these arrive, the tulip season is over for yet another year.

ABOVE Spaced well apart, Single Late tulips float above a mass of forget-me-nots in London's Kensington Gardens.

LEFT Triumphs 'Attila' and 'Arabian Mystery' and Single Late 'Queen of Night' rise above drifts of forget-me-nots and violets with, in the background, lighter tints provided by pink Triumphs 'Rosario', 'Meissner Porzellan' and 'White Dream'.

Tulipa acuminata
Miscellaneous tulips

Tulipa praestans
Miscellaneous tulips

'Ancilla'
Kaufmanniana Group tulips

'Purissima'
Fosteriana Group tulips

'Für Elise'
Greigii Group tulips

'Apricot Beauty'
Single Early Group tulips

'Monsella'
Double Early Group tulips

'Daydream'
Darwinhybrid Group tulips

'Negrita'
Triumph Group tulips

'Mrs John T. Scheepers'
Single Late Group tulips

'Picture'

'Queen of Night'

'Temple of Beauty'

'Colour Spectacle'
Multi-flowered tulips

'Red Shine'
Lily-flowered Group tulips

'Blue Heron'
Fringed Group tulips

'Spring Green'
Viridiflora Group tulips

'Black Parrot'
Parrot Group tulips

'Uncle Tom'
Double Late Group tulips

Tulipa sprengeri
Miscellaneous tulips

TWENTY CLASSIC TULIPS

In order to introduce the current asssortment of tulips, I have selected twenty of the best to act as guides. If you were to grow no others but these, you would have been exposed to the full spectrum of possibilities available today, but this is just the tip of an iceberg, with the current International Register of Tulip Names issued by the KAVB listing more than 2,600 varieties. With fewer than 10 per cent of these being regularly offered to gardeners, the problem of deciding what to grow may be reduced; however, it remains daunting. This and the following section of the book are designed to help.

Firstly, with the help of my twenty classic tulips, I introduce a selection of other good garden tulips, drawing from each of the fifteen different groups of tulip that make up the current international classification, with one exception, the Rembrandt Group, which are not in commercial production as the bulbs are infected with tulip breaking virus.

Secondly, from page 148 I look at tulips as a source of colour in the spring garden. We have already examined the many different types of plant that may already be occupying the garden in spring; armed with tulips we have the possibility of enhancing their effects by introducing either harmoniously coordinated varieties or vibrant contrasting colour schemes.

These two sections overlap in their coverage and should be used in conjunction with one another to identify the best cultivars and species for specific schemes in your garden.

'Red Shine' and 'Ballerina', two of the best Lily-flowered tulips

Tulipa acuminata

Miscellaneous tulips

Gardeners choose to grow plants for many different reasons. Sometimes their sumptuous blooms are enough: their colours, their form and even their scent will attract us. The associations we attach to certain plants may also be the reason we grow them. Memories of earlier encounters, associations with people or places, or historical events, are all good reasons that guide our plant selections. Tulips may qualify on all these counts and none more so for me than *Tulipa acuminata*.

This strange-shaped tulip is unique. The petals are drawn out to long thin points that claw wildly at the air surrounding them. Every flower is different, each fine twisted petal with its pale yellow base colour being splashed and streaked with irregular orange red markings. I can understand why some find its flowers wispy and misshapen, but this disorder is part of its attraction for me. Admittedly, in the open garden, its spidery flowers lack impact, but this can easily be overcome by good planting associations. However, of equal importance for me are the exotic associations and historical significance this extraordinary flower signals.

As I have already outlined, the spontaneous and unpredictable tulips, which are capable of transforming their colour and the form of their flowers to make a mockery of the botanists who try to classify them, have long captured the hearts and minds of all who appreciate their sensuous forms and ephemeral nature. Long before Carolus Clusius brought tulip bulbs to the Netherlands and triggered the Western obsession with these flowers, they had been grown and admired by the people living in the areas of the world where they originated and grew wild.

The Turkish fascination with the tulip reached its zenith during the reign of Ahmed III between 1703 and 1730, a period that is often referred to as the Tulip Era. The Sultan was obsessed with the tulip to the point that his subjects revolted at the unbridled extravagances of his annual tulip festivals. Accounts of the nightly parties in the gardens of the Grand Vizier (Ahmed's son-in-law) at Ciragan recall half a million tulips being supplemented by vases of still more from other gardens and nearby cutting fields; candles, lanterns and mirrors added to their spectacle, with song birds and musicians entertaining the colourfully clad guests throughout the night.

LEFT AND ABOVE
Tulipa acuminata

Tulipa acuminata gains impact in association with the Lily-flowered tulip 'Ballerina'.

By this time, the Dutch were exporting tulips and the Sultan's household was purchasing vast quantities to satisfy their obsession. These were of course not the highly prized dagger-shaped forms bred locally, the so-called Istanbul tulips, but the bowl-shaped flowers favoured in the West. At the peak of this era, huge prices were paid for the most prized Turkish varieties in a frenzy that closely recalled the tulip mania in the Netherlands some ninety years earlier. The government attempted to control the market by publishing official price lists, but the Tulip Era was nearing its close with the revolt that ended Ahmed's reign. Almost overnight the tulip lost its status and while its image continued to appear on Turkish textiles, carved stone and ceramics until the end of the eighteenth century its cultivation was abandoned.

During the Tulip Era the strange, etiolated flowers of Istanbul tulips were lovingly described in manuscripts that celebrated the achievements of eminent florists. Yet, surprisingly, there is only one known manuscript in which some of these celebrated cultivars are illustrated. This unique tome was probably made somewhere between 1725 and 1730. Its beautiful painted illustrations of forty-nine varieties depict incredibly shaped flowers, giving us just a glimpse into this special period of tulip history.

The tulip did not die out at the end of the Tulip Era of course, as by this time it was well established in European gardens, where its ability to capture men's hearts had already made its mark. To this day, the tulip still grows in the high passes of Central Asia and along the trade routes that chart the corridors taken by the expanding Ottoman Empire, its distribution for ever a record of its illustrious early history.

Tulipa acuminata is a poor substitute for the refined forms so revered in Turkey during the seventeenth and eighteenth centuries, but it is the nearest that we have. The plant has never been found growing in the wild and it is almost certainly of garden origin. Istanbul tulips were created by crossing not only species of Turkish origin but also imported species and cultivars from other regions. Today's *T. acuminata* is almost certainly the result of these crosses, but we will never really know for certain. This mystery adds to its allure while its writhing petals seem to point us back to a time in tulip history filled with excitement and exoticism. Memories of all this come into my mind when its flowers slowly unfold each spring in my garden. Perhaps one day I will build a garden kiosk hung with mirrors and lanterns, and surround it with these Istanbul tulips. Accompanying belly dancers, fire torches, and candles borne on the backs of roaming tortoises could all become a reality once more.

Tulipa acuminata needs to be grown in association with plants that enhance its garden impact. One approach would be to surround it with bold colourful foliage, as might be provided by the emerging leaves of purple-leaved *Ligularia dentata* and *Rheum palmatum*. My most successful association to date has been to mix it in equal quantities with the toffee-coloured tulip 'Ballerina'. This low-growing, Lily-flowered tulip picks up the colour splashes and streaks of the more delicate *T. acuminata*, while its pointed-petalled flowers make it seem like the modern representative of the lost Istanbul tulips. From a distance this combination registers as a splash of warm glowing orange that on closer inspection has a subtle combination of tints and forms with the added bonus of Ballerina's strong, sweet, evocative scent.

Neo-tulipae

The fact that *Tulipa acuminata* has never been found growing in the wild and is almost certainly of hybrid origin means that its name breaks the botanical rules of nomenclature for a plant species. A true species or not, rules are meant to be broken and what better to do it than an irascible tulip. Within the classification of tulips, *T. acuminata* is assigned to the Miscellaneous section. Here we find the true species tulips, plus a few other interlopers that, like *T. acuminata*, are of dubious origin. If, like me, your interest in a plant has as much to do with its history as its beauty, these oddities will have immediate appeal; three in particular are worthy of our attention, as they are also truly elegant and distinctive plants well worthy of garden space.

Tulipa didieri is a slim elegant tulip growing 16 inches/40 centimetres tall with currant red flowers. The petals are slender and slightly reflexed, adding considerably to its beauty. Inside, the base is blackish purple with a broad irregular cream white margin. It was first described in 1846, having been found growing in just two locations near Aime and Les Clappeys in the Savoy region of France near to the border with Italy. Subsequently building works destroyed the sites, but fortunately by then *T. didieri* had been brought into cultivation in the Netherlands by the bulb firm of C.G. van Tubergen and hence we can still enjoy it in our gardens today.

From the same region, *T. planifolia* is also worth acquiring. It is very similar to *T. didieri*, if not related to it, with large warm red flowers, a medley of pink orange and amber, and a yellow base. The pointed, slightly reflexed petals each bear an irregular black blotch.

Tulipa marjolletii was first described in 1894 and was found in the same alpine region of France. Such sites being so far from the normal distribution of tulip species and typically associated with agricultural activity gives weight to the assertion that these tulips do not represent truly wild populations. How they got there, who was involved and which species were their true ancestors we will never know. The plants, however, resemble small delicate forms of modern-day cultivars and are ideally suited to intimate spaces in our gardens where their modest scale seems appropriate. With their status as true species in question, these European forms are referred to collectively as the Neo-tulipae, a unique group to cherish and cosset.

T. marjolletii is 16 inches/40 centimetres tall with soft creamy yellow flowers. The petals are finely edged and streaked with dark cerise red, which increases as the flowers mature while their yellow tint fades to white. Flowering time is very late, around the end of May in the Netherlands, putting it in competition with *T. sprengeri* for the title of the last tulip to flower each season.

Tulipa marjolletii

Tulipa planifolia

Tulipa praestans

Miscellaneous tulips: early-flowering species

All the tulip cultivars we can grow today share their origins with the wild populations of species growing on the plains and in the mountains of Central Asia. Adapted to the arid conditions of their homelands, many of the species tulips are low in stature. In their natural conditions the bulbs are located deep in the ground, which is porous and well drained, and they require full exposure to the sun both when in leaf and flower as well as throughout their resting period. None of this promises plants capable of having an impact in our gardens or thriving in average garden soil, especially during our long damp winters in northern Europe. Nevertheless, tulips are tough and adaptable plants and within their many variations a large number of species and their cultivars have been found that will grow happily in garden conditions. Naturally, well-drained soil in a position fully exposed to sunshine is essential for them.

Collectors may wish to cherish diminutive species in the rock garden or in pots in the alpine house, but in the open garden we need plants with stature and bold colouration if they are to justify their position. The exquisite

jewel-like qualities of many readily available species such as *Tulipa biflora, T. schrenkii, T. polychroma* and *T. turkestanica* lead me to grow them as pot plants in my cold greenhouse, but outside in the garden I find my choice limited to just a handful of other species.

Tulipa praestans is top of my list on two counts. Firstly, it flowers very early, sometimes during the second half of March in the Netherlands, and secondly, it is multi-flowered, creating a bold splash of colour wherever it is used. It is not the first species to come into flower, but it is the first with dramatic impact, albeit in a neck-and-neck race for this title with the early-flowering Kaufmanniana tulips such as 'The First' and 'Stresa', and these, indeed, can make ideal companions for it. The orange scarlet flowers begin to show themselves when it is only just emerging from the soil, but quickly they are lifted to nearly 12 inches/30 centimetres high. Each bulb produces between three and six flowers to create a bunch of vibrant colour that becomes effective over a considerable distance. The best selection of this species is *T. praestans* 'Fusilier' with five or six rounded flowers of an intense carrot orange

Tulipa clusiana

Tulipa humilis Albocaerulea
Oculata Group

colouration. 'Van Tubergen's Variety' is often substituted for the true 'Fusilier' by less worthy traders; it has fewer, more pointed, redder-coloured flowers, but its greater height (to nearly 12 inches/30 centimetres) is its advantage. 'Zwanenburg Variety' is likewise red and there are various other selections which may from time to time be offered in bulb catalogues. Having seen them grown side by side in trial fields, I cannot say that the differences are all that great, but 'Fusilier' is possibly the most refined. One selection that does stand out, however, is 'Unicum', which has boldly variegated creamy yellow leaf margins. Even before it comes into flower, the foliage attracts attention and reminds me of small, variegated hosta plants precociously emerging from the soil.

A few bulbs of *Tulipa praestans* go a long way and I grow mine in the narrow strips of soil either side of the path leading to my front door. Here also snowdrops will have just finished their subtle display as the first of these tulips come into flower. Cold temperatures tend to extend flowering periods and, with luck, they will remain effective until the middle of the following month. Behind them taller-growing Botanical tulips derived from *T. kaufmanniana, T. fosteriana* and *T. greigii* contribute to the show along with some Single Early tulips.

There is a group of early-flowering tulips that, in spite of their small size, have found their way into my garden borders. *T. humilis* typically begins to flower even earlier than *T. praestans*, but it works well with it, especially the darker-coloured forms of this exciting species, which in form and function reminds me of the better-known crocus. Unlike crocus, the long spidery foliage is inconspicuous below the open flowers with pointed petals and contrasting base colours. The selections made from wild populations generally grow 4 inches/10 centimetres tall while some of the cultivars can achieve 6 inches/15 centimetres in ideal conditions. Again, these little tulips give botanists problems and result in various names appearing in bulb catalogues. *T. humilis, T. pulchella* and *T. violacea* have all been used in

the past, but at present *T. humilis* is being used to describe all of them, with *T.h.* var. *pulchella* and *T.h.* Violacea Group being used to distinguish between them.

Wild *T. humilis* is found in shades of pink through to white with a clear yellow base. More exciting are a group of multi-flowered cultivars of intense colouration. 'Lilliput' is cardinal red with a violet base; 'Pegasus' is glowing fuchsia pink and purple with a muddy yellow base; and 'Zephyr' is blood red with a black base.

T. humilis Albocaerulea Oculata Group is far more subtle, with pointed white petals and a steel blue base. In reality, this is one for the alpine specialist as it is difficult to grow and flower well and would be quite ineffective in a garden border. However, it might be considered one of the most exquisite of all tulips and therefore one I cannot exclude from these pages.

The most popular cultivar, *T. humilis* Violacea Group black base has glorious goblet-shaped, purple cherry pink flowers up to 6 inches/15 centimetres tall with a dark mustard brown base that bears an indistinct yellow edge. Its popularity means that the bulbs are reasonably priced, making it the best choice for mass planting to create bold splashes of early spring colour. Next to my carrot orange *T. praestans* it recalls memories of pop art imagery from the early 1960s. The largest-flowered form of all is the cultivar *T.h.* 'Magenta Queen'. It is paler, violet pink with a green outer flame and a yellow base, but unfortunately it increases very slowly and is therefore quite expensive.

The form *T.h.* Violacea Group yellow base and its cultivars are smaller than the black-based forms, their leaves are narrower, the flowers are more star-like and the yellow base has no surrounding edge. 'Persian Pearl' is distinctive with rich magenta pink flowers and a pale greenish outer flame on its outer three petals. 'Odalisque' is dark brownish red contrasting with a large canary yellow base. 'Eastern Star', with magenta pink flowers with a bronze green outer flame, is the last of the whole group of *T. humilis* to flower.

The earliest-flowering tulips may not be the most dramatic, but they have a subtle beauty that makes them well worth growing in pots or in small pockets in the rock garden. *T. biflora* is multi-flowered with small white flowers with yellow bases. *T. turkestanica* is the tetraploid form (see page 109) and as a consequence is larger and more robust. The star-shaped flowers, held 8–10 inches/20–25 centimetres high, are white with a discreet violet purple blush on the outside and a bold orange yellow base. The leaves are long and straggly and it increases freely by both bulbils and stolons. It grows easily and may spread too quickly in a rock garden. This problem can be avoided and flowering improved by restricting its root run with stones or tiles. The other similar early-flowering species is *T. polychroma* and this is my favourite of the three. Although only 4–5 inches/10–12 centimetres tall, its clear white flowers have bold yellow bases and on the outside the petals are delicately flamed in pinkish purple. This charming plant is probably a variant of *T. biflora*, but is quite distinctive and exquisite when seen close to, growing in a pot.

There is one more classic species tulip that any serious gardener should know, the slim and perfectly formed lady tulip or more correctly *T. clusiana*. It flowers a little later than the other species mentioned so far, it grows 10 inches/25 centimetres tall, the leaves are held upright, as are the flowers, which are pure white with a broad carmine red mark on the three outer petals, and the base is violet. Everything about this plant is elegant and poised. It is not one for creating bold splashes of colour, but rather to be grown in discrete clumps in prominent positions where it can receive all the attention it deserves. Clusius records receiving it and seeing it in flower for the first time in 1607. It forms stolons and often spreads around without flowering, but following a long hot summer it quickly regains one's admiration.

There are a number of cultivars regularly offered for sale and all tend to be stronger growing than the true species. The flowers of *T. clusiana* 'Cynthia' appear orange from a distance; they are reddish outside and bright

Tulipa humilis 'Persian Pearl'

Tulipa humilis Violacea Group black base

Tulipa praestans 'Fusilier'

Tulipa polychroma

yellow within, with some orange streaking. *T.c.* var. *chrysantha* is bolder with deep yellow flowers and bold red outer markings. The form *T.c.* var. *chrysantha* 'Tubergen's Gem' is preferable as its flowers are slightly larger and most importantly it is stronger growing. In all honesty, only the pure red and white species appeals to me; these red and yellow forms fail to compete with other vibrant bicoloured Kaufmanniana and Single Early tulips which I would rather grow in my garden. However, as pot plants their scale is more appropriate and they could be used to add height and contrast to a collection of other pot-grown tulip species.

'ANCILLA'

Kaufmanniana Group tulips

Short in stature, with long-petalled flowers that open into wide stars in sunshine, 'Ancilla' is typical of the Kaufmanniana Group of tulips, which are often referred to as the waterlily tulips. Although a few species have already flowered in the rock garden or the alpine house, it is with the flowering of *Tulipa kaufmanniana* and its many cultivars that the tulip season in the open garden can be said to have really started.

Ancilla has ivory cream petals with a bold carmine red flame on the outside, but when fully open all attention is drawn to the bright yellow base and its scarlet ring markings. As these flowers age they become suffused with pink and you need to bear this in mind when placing them in the garden.

Kaufmanniana Group tulips are one of three divisions in the official classification commonly referred to as Botanical tulips. The wild species and its cultivars bear a close resemblance to one another and together are supposed to represent a coherent group. Typically, Kaufmanniana tulips bear broad leaves nestling close to the ground and the short flower stems carry their long-petalled flowers never more than 8 inches/20 centimetres above them. The comparison with a waterlily arises from the way the flowers open out in full sunshine until almost flat, closing up again each evening and only partially opening in overcast weather. When fully open, these dynamic blooms may exceed 10 inches/25 centimetres in diameter, creating bold spreads of colour that seem to float across the garden floor.

Grouped together, waterlily tulips such as 'Ancilla' form uniform pools of colour which would be disturbed by interplanting them with other plants and certainly anything taller that would disturb their horizontal plane. They are most effective, therefore, when mass planted as contiguous drifts through and behind wider patches of lower-growing perennial ground covers or spring-flowering bulbs such as *Scilla bifolia* and *S. siberica*.

Flowering so early in the year, these tulips are susceptible to damage from hail and storms. You should grow them in sheltered positions or in pots which you can move temporarily inside when inclement weather threatens. Ideally, the soil should be deep and well draining. When happy, they may be left in the ground and will not only reappear in subsequent years but also increase in numbers. If instead you decide to lift

LEFT AND ABOVE 'Ancilla'

'Corona'

'Early Harvest'

'Franz Léhar'

'Fritz Kreisler'

the bulbs in order to store them during the summer, you will need to dig deeply as they may produce their new bulbs on the ends of droppers (extension growths) well below the depth of the mother bulbs.

Tulipa kaufmanniana was described in 1877 by Dr Eduard August von Regel from the plants he had collected on the rocky slopes of the Tien Shan mountains of Turkistan near the Chirchik River. Although in the wild the species exhibits considerable variation of form and flower colour, the only type in cultivation is a single clone with flowers that are creamy white inside, deepening near the base to yellow; with an intermediate dull red band, the backs of the outer three petals have a carmine red blush. In bulb catalogues this form is usually listed as the 'type' species.

Through hybridization with other species, the colour range of the Kaufmanniana cultivars has been considerably enhanced and, with the influence of *T. greigii,* many of these cultivars possess attractively mottled leaf patterns.

The pioneering bulb firm of C.G. van Tubergen was responsible for bringing to the market the first Kaufmanniana hybrid selections in the 1920s and 1930s, and F. Rijnveld & Sons of Hillegom introduced still more in the 1960s. Since then, in spite of their usefulness to gardeners, the introduction of new cultivars has declined. In part, this can be explained by the fact that they rarely produce sports, which is the source of new cultivars in many of the other tulip classes. More significantly, however, the hybridization of Kaufmannianas has virtually stopped with the increasing economic value of the forcing market for cut flowers in which these short-stemmed tulips have no place.

'The First', although often coming at the end of any alphabetical list of Kaufmannianas, is true to its name by being one of the very earliest to come into flower. It is a robust cultivar, very similar to the type species, but with a stronger stem, which means that it is less easily damaged by strong winds. The outer three petals are carmine red, edged white. Inside, the flower is ivory white with a yellow base and yellow anthers. It was registered by F. Roozen in 1940.

'Johann Strauss' is very similar, but later flowering. One of the most popular cultivars, it has the added attraction of purple-streaked foliage. In this respect the cultivar 'Franz Léhar' is particularly noteworthy, its glaucous blue leaves being boldly striped purple. Its pink and pale sulphur yellow flowers are delicate and best appreciated when grown as a pot plant. In the border it can bring pools of light to otherwise dark recesses.

The smaller-flowered 'Heart's Delight' is deservedly popular. Its flowers, officially described as carmine red on the outside with a pale rose edge and interior, fade gradually to a gentle pink as they mature. Its delicate, dare I say feminine appearance often seems at odds with its presence in the tough blustery days of early spring and to me it always looks better grown in pots situated in an enclosed, protected courtyard.

In contrast to the cultivars so far described, 'Ancilla' is bolder and more effective from a distance. Amongst the earliest of its group to flower, 'Ancilla' would be my first choice to bring light into the bare recesses of a dormant shrub border.

'Early Harvest' is slightly taller growing at 10 inches/25 centimetres and heads the next group of Kaufmanniana tulips, all of which possess far bolder and more dramatic flower colours. 'Early Harvest' possesses all the qualities we expect from a good Kaufmanniana cultivar. It flowers very early, just after 'The First'; it is robust, surviving blustery weather well; and it is vigorous, producing offsets freely. The flowers are a rich medley of oranges and russets; bold without being brash. Registered by F. Rijnveld & Sons in 1966, it has since won many awards including the Award of Garden Merit from the Royal Horticultural Society in 1993.

'Love Song' arose in the same batch of seedlings as 'Early Harvest' and is remarkably similar. The outside of the petals is a slightly darker red, officially mandarin red, which radiates through the open flowers giving them a richer, warmer appearance.

'Shakespeare' was registered by C.G. van Tubergen in 1942. The waterlily flower shape is beautifully proportioned and its warm salmon colour arises from the combined effects of the carmine red exterior petals edged with salmon and the salmon-flushed scarlet interior plus the golden base. While this is an excellent garden tulip, it has been almost entirely replaced in the trade by the newer and far more vigorous cultivar 'Fashion', which you should avoid at all costs: 'Fashion' is a poor substitute for 'Shakespeare' as its weak flowers are easily damaged and rarely last more than a couple of days in the open garden.

Also registered in the same year (1962), 'Scarlet Baby' has an elegant flower. It is an even geranium red on the outside and scarlet on the inside. The bright yellow base is not bordered by any other colour, unlike so many of the others.

'Goudstuk' is the best of another group of Kaufmanniana tulips sometimes described as bicolours. These tulips have a broad splash of red applied to the outside of their bold yellow flowers. 'Stresa' is by far the most freely available of these rather brash-coloured tulips and would be the one to go for in a mass bedding scheme. I love it and use it freely in my own garden, where it seems to shout out that spring has finally arrived. 'Goudstuk' forms a large plant, 12 inches/30 centimetres tall, with bigger flowers. Unfortunately, the bulbs increase slowly, making it expensive and difficult to obtain. The contrast between the exterior carmine red blotch and the

yellow edge and interior of 'Giuseppe Verdi' is in comparison far less strident. It is a robust and persistent tulip and would be the better choice for the less formal parts of a garden; 'Johann Strauss' and 'Glück' are both paler yellow and lightly marked in comparison and consequently far less strident, but nevertheless highly desirable.

'Corona', red on the outside and pale yellow inside, reveals a distinctive scarlet ring around the centre of its flowers when they are fully open. It is far less brash than many of the other bicolours but sufficiently bright to make its mark in the open garden landscape. 'Berlioz' is even more effective, opening its red-backed flowers to reveal wide plates of stronger lemon yellow surrounding a golden base. With broad attractively mottled foliage, it is considered to be one of the most beautiful of all, but rarely do you find it being offered for sale.

'Showwinner' is the ultimate Kaufmanniana tulip where early season colour is a priority. It has indeed won many awards. The foliage is thick, wide and attractively marked, it is robust and vigorous, but, above all else, it is the colour that sets it apart: deep cardinal red on the outside, signal red inside with a buttercup yellow base. When F. Rijnveld & Sons registered it in 1966 it was praised as one of their best-ever cultivars. Its status has stood the test of time.

'Giuseppe Verdi'

'Johann Strauss'

'Shakespeare'

'Showwinner'

'Stresa'

'PURISSIMA'

Fosteriana Group tulips

Many gardeners regard 'Purissima' as the best white tulip ever bred. It is certainly a classy tulip, but whether or not you consider its creamy blooms white or yellow is highly subjective. This Botanical tulip is a member of the dramatic Fosteriana Group, which start flowering slightly later than the Kaufmanniana tulips, their seasons overlapping from around the beginning of April. 'Purissima' is 18 inches/45 centimetres tall. Its flowers have broad elongated petals surrounding a yellow base and unusually for this group it is scented.

Tulipa fosteriana was first collected in Central Asia by Joseph Haberhauer in 1902 for the Dutch bulb firm C.G. van Tubergen. From the first consignments which arrived in Holland in around 1906 two selections are still in cultivation: 'Princeps' with broad wide-spreading leaves and a very short flower stem, and the well-known 'Madame Lefeber', with spectacular flowers as much as 10 inches/25 centimetres across.

What was remarkable about these tulips when they first arrived in Europe was the intensity of their red flowers and their great size. Since then Fosteriana tulips have played a significant role in many hybridization programmes. 'Madame Lefeber' in particular has been used repeatedly, being crossed with *T. kaufmanniana* and its hybrids, Single Early tulips and most significantly the Darwin tulips to produce the phenomenally successful group, the Darwinhybrids.

Times move on and for more than forty years no attempts were made in Holland to breed new Fosteriana tulips. Market economics were at the heart of this lull as the Fosteriana tulips were seen as simply less important than tulips more suited for forcing as cut flowers. With the vigour of many of the older varieties now waning, the range and quality of Fosteriana tulips on the market declines yearly. However, with Botanical tulips as a group becoming increasingly important to landscape architects, who have started to incorporate them into extensive permanent planting schemes, demand is on the increase. This in turn has prompted breeders of new varieties to rectify the current situation, and exciting new hybrids, including vigorous tetraploid crosses (see page 109), are in the pipeline. While we might eagerly anticipate the release of these in the coming years, the current assortment still offers us some indispensable garden tulips and fortunately some of these have,

LEFT A mixture of 'Purissima', 'Orange Emperor' and two-toned yellow 'Easter Moon' with its variegated foliage

ABOVE 'Purissima'

'Candela'

'Dance'

'Juan'

in recent years, produced sports which have usefully extended the colour range.

Fosteriana tulips might be used in the garden to take over from the earliest-flowering Kaufmanniana tulips or be selected to provide the first main splash of colour of the gardening year. They are popular in public parks and gardens, where their greater height and bold colours afford them increased impact. In common with the other Botanical tulips, Fosteriana tulips can behave like perennials when planted deeply. In my own garden, with far from ideal soil conditions, the yellow and white 'Sweetheart' has reappeared in the same place for more than six years.

'Madame Lefeber' remains popular on account of its bold fiery red flowers, which have a black base edged with yellow. It grows 16 inches/40 centimetres tall but the stems are weaker than we might hope for, and in wet and windy weather the display is all too easily damaged. This trait has unfortunately been passed on to some of its many offspring; however, one of the best, 'Orange Emperor', has avoided the problem.

'Orange Emperor' has flowers that are a strident carrot orange on the outside, paler on the inside, with a pale buttercup yellow base and contrasting dark black anthers. The colour is sophisticated rather than brash, even though the flowers can glow brightly when backlit by low-angled sunlight. It grows 16 inches/40 centimetres tall and is never subject to wind damage; a truly indispensable tulip that can be grown anywhere. 'Orange Brilliant' is similar with possibly slightly richer-toned flowers.

'Purissima', being less colourful, is far more easily placed in the garden landscape. The white flowers are held clear of its healthy grey green foliage by strong stems some 18 inches/45 centimetres high. This vigorous, easily grown tulip will be in flower for up to three weeks in the middle of the tulip season and is extremely useful for associations with a host of other mid-season tulips from the Triumph and Darwinhybrid groups. 'Purissima' has produced a number of equally valuable sports: 'Yellow Purissima', a strong lemon yellow with a canary yellow edge; 'Golden Purissima', a darker richer

yellow; and 'Purissima King', which is red with a yellow base. 'Flaming Purissima' is a more recent introduction with a creamy white base colour overlaid with pink that intensifies towards the edges of the petals.

'Madame Lefeber', 'Purissima' and 'Yellow Purissima' are often called 'Red Emperor', 'White Emperor' and 'Yellow Emperor' respectively, even though none of these names is valid. Together with 'Orange Emperor' these names have helped market this strong healthy group of gardenworthy tulips.

'Sweetheart' arose as a sport of an unnamed Fosteriana hybrid that had become mixed up with a batch of 'Purissima'. The barium yellow petals fade to white at their tips, giving the impression of a foaming glass of Dutch lager. Although it comes into flower slightly later than 'Purissima' and 'Yellow Purissima', it can still be mixed with them to make a medley of springtime yellows. It also associates well with the petite Jonquilla daffodil Narcissus 'Pipit' with its comparable colour scheme of lemon yellow petals surrounding a white trumpet. 'Sweetheart' is an attractive cultivar that has become increasingly popular since its introduction in 1976. 'Easter Moon' is similar, with two-toned primrose-yellow flowers and vigorous upright foliage crisply edged creamy yellow. It was registered in 1996 by J.N.M. van Eeden, and being a sport of 'Yellow Purissima' shares its health and vigour.

The old pure yellow cultivar 'Candela' has to some extent been superseded in the bulb catalogues by 'Yellow Purissima'. However, its colour is slightly deeper and at only 15 inches/35 centimetres tall it might, in certain situations, be the more appropriate choice.

Not all the Fosteriana tulips are as tall as the 'Emperors' and for that reason they are less useful in the open garden where, by mid-spring, they can be easily overshadowed by other border plants. These shorter cultivars, which often remind me of the earlier-flowering Kaufmannianas, are probably best used in pots or in discrete clumps in the rock garden. 'Princeps' is one of the original selections from the wild species; it flowers early mid season in the same glowing red as 'Madame Lefeber' but only reaches 8 inches/20 centimetres tall. More typical of the group I am describing here, 'Dance' is around 8 inches/20 centimetres tall with flowers that are pink on the outside, white inside and have a black centre bordered by a broad brilliant scarlet band. The yellow stamens complete what must be the most beautiful centre of any tulip flower we can grow today.

'Concerto' is pale sulphur yellow, both outside and in, with a broad yellow band around its dark base. 'Salut' is similar, but with pink flushes on the outside of the flowers and some pink streaking in the less colourful yellow band around its dark base. 'Zombie' at 15 inches/35 centimetres is slightly taller than these two. It has pale–yellow–tinted flowers with a more noticeable cerise outer flame and a bright red edge to its dark base.

One unique Fosteriana tulip to know is 'Cantata', which flowers some two weeks earlier than most others in its group. It is similarly low growing, at around 12 inches/30 centimetres, with its earlier season meaning that it can still be effective in the open garden at a time when very little else has started into growth. It is compact with distinctive glossy apple green leaves. The vivid orange scarlet flowers are tempered by a buff, bronze-like flush down the middle of each of its petals, making it both bold yet sophisticated. Unfortunately, 'Cantata' is losing its vigour and disappearing rapidly from commercial production. Breeders are hoping that some of the new hybrids will fill its unique place in the assortment in the coming years.

Some of the Fosteriana tulips have been created by hybridization with *T. greigii* and its cultivars, resulting in the inheritance of beautiful dramatically striped leaves. Popular 'Juan', 18 inches/45 centimetres tall, and the slightly shorter and consequently sturdier 'Toulon' are possibly more interesting as foliage plants than when in bloom. For my taste, their bold orange red flowers with a splash of yellow at the base are too strident for the open garden and are much better seen as specimen pot-grown plants. I must admit, however, that with their bold foliage display long before the flowers appear they make an excellent choice for mass bedding in public spaces.

'Madame Lefeber'

Tulipa 'Orange Emperor' and *Narcissus* 'Flower Record'

'Sweetheart'

'Yellow Purissima' and 'Purissima' with Cyclamineus narcissus 'Jenny'

'FÜR ELISE'

Greigii Group tulips

The flower colour of 'Für Elise' is a complex mixture of apricot, yellow and pink and its foliage is lightly mottled. This Greigii tulip was registered in 1986 and it has been welcome in my garden ever since, not only because of its elegant flower shape but also and especially for its subtle, soft colouration. I mix tulips with perennials in my borders and since 'Für Elise' is only 12 inches/30 centimetres tall it must be given a position near the front. This can lead to problems after flowering when its foliage needs to be left to die down naturally; however, for such a desirable tulip I am prepared to make an exception.

Gardening is all about satisfying needs and making choices. Often this goes no further than the desire to grow something we have read about or seen. As a designer, I am constantly analysing plants in order to identify ways of utilizing their specific characteristics to create garden effects. In spite of their popularity and evident appeal, it is when I try to decide how to use Greigii tulips in the garden that I encounter problems that do not seem to apply to most of the other groups of tulips – or at least not in the majority of cases.

Greigii tulips are the last of the three so-called Botanical tulips to flower, the majority of them flowering in April and some on into the beginning of May. Because, like 'Für Elise', most do not exceed 16 inches/40 centimetres in height, their use in mixed borders in combination with perennials in particular can lead to problems; all too easily they become submerged in the burgeoning foliage of their neighbours.

A second problem relates to Greigii hybrids being highly distinguished tulips. Their broad, often wavy leaves are boldly marked with purple/brown stripes and stipples and their flashy flowers are large, often reflexed open and richly coloured. Some of the most beautiful cultivars have bold bicoloured blooms: 'Cape Cod', for example, which is reddish apricot edged yellow with a narrow streak of apricot down the middle of the petals on the inside. These jewel-like Greigiis are individuals to be carefully studied and enjoyed at close quarters, and not the sort of plants for creating bold effects in the open landscape or for mass bedding – a use for which they are so often recommended. A formal bed of Greigii tulips

'Calypso'

'Dreamboat'

'Easter Surprise'

'Flowerdale'

always appears stiff to my eyes, the plants seeming too self-conscious with each individual craving the spotlight.

This characteristic is, however, perfectly suited to their use in small discrete clumps in the rock garden, where they also find the well-drained soil and summer baking they need to ripen their bulbs for the following year. But not many modern gardens have a large rock garden appropriate for displaying these bold individuals. However, pots and containers abound, and it is here that the Greigiis seem to have found their place in today's gardens.

These hybrids do not grow well in heavy clay soils; they much prefer a well-drained loam, moist throughout the growing season and bone dry in summer. Although this applies to most tulips, the Greigiis are a particular favourite of slugs, which make a beeline for their broad, low-growing and apparently very tasty leaves. This is yet another reason why they are more successful when grown in pots.

Tulipa greigii was first described by Dr Eduard August von Regel in 1873 from plants collected a few years earlier in Turkistan. Although C.G. van Tubergen received bulbs around the same time, it was not until 1950 that the firm began to register any hybrids. In the wild, the species is highly variable. The leaves are broad and may be dramatically undulated, but all, to some degree, are marked with purple or brown dots or stripes. The flowers range from red through orange to bicoloured forms; some are even cream. Most, in common with all other species of tulips, have six petals; however, sometimes plants with eight petals are encountered.

'Margaret Herbst' was one of the earliest and best cultivars to be introduced. It was produced by Dirk Lefeber, who after various attempts created a series of hybrids using 'City of Haarlem', a Darwin tulip that is no longer in cultivation. The flowers of 'Margaret Herbst' are clear vermilion red and the leaves beautifully marked. It is unusually tall for a Greigii at 20 inches/50 centimetres, which makes it a far more useful cultivar than many. In 1989 its yellow sport 'Lemon Giant' was registered by W.A.M. Pennings. This is an equally tall and useful plant.

'Oriental Splendour' came from the same breeding programme as 'Margaret Herbst', even though it was not registered until 1961. It is equally vigorous and tall, with petals that are carmine red, yellow edged on the outside and lemon yellow inside with a red ring surrounding the green basal blotch. It has produced one sport called 'Imperial Splendour'.

'Compostella' is more typical of the Greigii Group as a whole. It is 10 inches/25 centimetres tall, flowering in April and May. Its flowers are a complex mixture of red tints with fine yellow-edged petals plus a black basal blotch inside. Sometimes more than one dramatic flower per bulb is produced. The leaves are striped purple.

'Easter Surprise' has a combination of colours that never cease to attract me. Its deep lemon yellow petals become orange towards their edges, creating a flower that seems to radiate heat. It grows no more than 15 inches/35 centimetres high and would make a harmonious partner for the taller-growing Fosteriana tulip 'Orange Emperor' which flowers at about the same time. Here maybe is a Greigii that I will one day let loose into my herbaceous borders.

'Red Riding Hood' (Roodkapje) is probably the best known of all the Greigii Group. At only 8 inches/20 centimetres tall it is smaller and shorter than many, but the combination of richly marked leaves and clear carmine red square flowers sets it apart. This is the perfect container plant for providing a splash of mid-season colour.

'Orange Elite' is a very bold and distinctive cultivar. Its flowers are a striking orange blended with apricot and rose on the outside. It cannot be used just anywhere, but with moderation it can be relied upon to inject drama to the scene; for sheer impact there are few tulips that can compete. I once encountered discrete clumps of eight to twelve plants surrounded by a mass of clear blue grape hyacinths (*Muscari armeniacum*) and the effect was stunning (see page 54). It grows 15 inches/35 centimetres tall and has attractively marked foliage, although the large flowers tend to dominate.

'Toronto' is deservedly popular. While some of the Greigiis throw up an extra couple of flowers from time to time, 'Toronto' is a truly multi-flowered cultivar so long as you plant the largest bulbs (size 12); otherwise it will remain single. It produces three to five relatively smaller blooms per bulb, which tend to develop successively, thereby extending its flowering period. The flowers are salmon pink fading to pale yellow at their base and it grows to about 15 inches/35 centimetres tall. 'Toronto' is tough and easy, growing almost anywhere in the garden, and fortunately it is less susceptible to slug attack than most. It has produced two equally valuable sports over the years: 'Orange Toronto' in 1987 and 'Quebec' in 1991, which has scarlet flowers edged by a broad yellow green band.

Many of the most dramatic Greigiis are bicolours. 'Cape Cod' is apricot orange edged with yellow, as mentioned earlier; 'Golden Day' is red edged with yellow; 'Plaisir' is red edged with sulphur; and 'Pinocchio' is similar in red edged with white. I have never wanted to grow any of these in the garden although I can see their appeal as pot specimens.

Pink-flowered Greigiis are the most refined members of the group. 'Perlina' is a rich pink with a lemon yellow base; 'Sweet Lady' is a warmer pink with a bronze green base; but undoubtedly my favourite is 'Dreamboat', which has an amber yellow flower flamed red to create its glowing pink-effect blooms. 'Oratorio' is similar with extremely attractive foliage.

The choice of Greigii tulips increases every year. One that has caught my attention recently is 'Flowerdale'; it has just started to appear in bulb catalogues. It only grows 10 inches/25 centimetres tall, but its 6 inch/15 centimetre wide star-shaped flowers are golden yellow and heavily flamed dark red creating a vibrant rich warm glow. Like the Kaufmanniana tulips, this is one to use in spreading groups to create pools of colour in garden situations where it can be seen from a distance.

'Plaisir'

'Quebec'

'Red Riding Hood'

'Sweet Lady'

'Toronto'

'APRICOT BEAUTY'

Single Early Group tulips

Just as *Tulipa acuminata* is one of the least typical of all tulips, in many ways 'Apricot Beauty' might qualify as one of the most typical. Its egg-shaped buds open to single round-cupped flowers with short round-ended petals. However, this typical tulip is also exceptional on account of its unique colour. The official colour description of salmon rose tinged with red hardly does justice to its subtle combination of peach and pink reminiscent of lightly blushing skin. It has a radiance that sets it apart from any of the clear pink tulips such as 'Pink Diamond' and 'Queen of Bartigons'. Oozing femininity, this sumptuously coloured flower has sufficient depth to allow it to play a contrasting role in a wide range of colour schemes.

The yellow side of this tulip's character suggests combinations with copper and purples, as can be found in the foliage of heucheras, epimediums and *Tellima grandiflora*. As it flowers through the second half of April, appropriate combinations may be found with equally early-flowering primulas, polyanthus and violas in shades of pale yellow, copper, orange, darker mahogany and maroon. The chartreuse tints of early-flowered spurges such as *Euphorbia*

amygdaloides var. *robbiae* can introduce a sharper note to such combinations. Alternatively, the rose red tints in the flowers of 'Apricot Beauty' suggest contrasting combinations with blues and purples. As we have seen, blue flowers abound at this time on biennial forget-me-nots (*Myosotis*), perennials such as pulmonarias, brunneras and omphalodes, and numerous bulbs such as grape hyacinths (*Muscari*), scillas and chionodoxas. Some of the mid-season-flowering tulips, especially Triumphs such as 'Attila' and 'Passionale' in shades of violet purple, will also overlap their flowering seasons and work extremely well. *Clematis alpina* is usually in flower at the same time in my garden and, had I space in the narrow border in front of the low fence it drapes, it would make a perfect background with its smoky blue hanging bells.

'Apricot Beauty' is classified as a Single Early tulip and there will be other members of the class flowering at the same time, although it is a little bit later than many of them. 'Bestseller' and 'Beauty Queen', being sports of 'Apricot Beauty', will always flower at the same time. The former is a more brightly coloured version of its parent, while 'Beauty Queen' is predominantly

'Beauty Queen' (and 'Entertainer')

'Bestseller'

'Christmas Dream'

'Christmas Marvel'

pink, with words such as rose, salmon and shrimp appearing in its official description. All three of these could be used in association with one another in a larger border planting scheme.

'Apricot Beauty' and its sports are less robust than most other members of the Single Early Group of tulips and this comes about through the way the group has been assembled over the years. Significantly the Duc van Tol tulips are now included in the group. The earliest of these litle tulips, 'Duc van Tol Red and Yellow', dates from 1595 and is the oldest tulip in the historic collection at the Hortus Bulborum in the Netherlands. Most of those still in existence date from c.1700. No longer in commercial productivity, they were important in breeding programmes to create early-flowering hybrids. When they were crossed with the taller-growing Darwin tulips the Mendel Group arose. For a time these were the dominant forcing tulip. However, they had small flowers and weak stems and were eventually superseded by the sturdier Triumph tulips that dominate the cut flower sector today.

'Apricot Beauty' was once classified as a Mendel tulip and shares their weaker constitution. Perhaps this affirms its femininity, but it means that it needs to be grown in a

sheltered spot away from the worst of the wind and rain. In a pot it could be brought under cover during a storm, but in the open garden it should not be relied upon for the dominant display, but rather be used in carefully chosen associations highlighting its unrivalled colouration.

Tulips now classified as Single Early should begin flowering before the middle of April in the Netherlands. With cool temperatures these tough tulips can still be in flower in early May, so take care to avoid colour clashes with mid- and late-season-flowering tulips with whose season they may overlap. Averaging 12–16 inches/30–40 centimetres in height with brightly coloured flowers on sturdy stems, these are extremely versatile in the open garden, as they will withstand most that the weather can throw at them. Ideal for early mass bedding schemes, they also work well as drifts and clumps amongst the newly emerging perennials in herbaceous borders. Especially in situations where their leafy presence would be a problem in early summer, these early-flowering types can be tidied away in time to leave space for adjacent plants to expand or to make room for planting summer-flowering annuals.

Some fine old cultivars are still offered commercially even though they are no longer of interest to cut flower growers. Their age gives an indication of their toughness and I have found that they reappear each spring without being lifted for summer storage above ground. 'Keizerskroon' is one of the oldest cultivars still in commercial cultivation, having first been recorded in 1750. It is not subtle: the scarlet red outer petals are edged deeply in bright yellow.

'Generaal de Wet', registered in 1904, is a glowing soft amber which on closer inspection can be seen to be produced by a network of rich orange streaks upon a yellow ground. It would be hard to find a situation where this colour would not fit and when its open cup-shaped flowers release their sweet fragrance it is one of my favourite early-spring flowers. It is a sport of 'Prince of Austria' (Prins van Oostenrijk), which dates back to 1860 and is still occasionally listed in bulb catalogues. In every way it is similar to 'Generaal de Wet' apart from the colour, which is a darker glowing orange red. Of course they look wonderful grown together, but it would also work in the same types of combination suggested for 'Apricot Beauty', which it would also go with.

Another 'Prince of Austria' sport, called 'Prins Carnaval', registered in 1930, is a slight improvement over 'Keizerskroon'. Here the yellow edges to the scarlet flowers are a softer shade, giving the flowers a cleaner, fresher look. In 1960 'Mickey Mouse' arrived and it has become a popular cut flower, but its colours are harder and there is no scent, so my advice would be to seek out the older cultivars even though they will cost slightly more effort and money to acquire.

'Flair' (1978) is a Single Early tulip that refuses to be ignored, and at times I can see the appeal. It has broad buttercup yellow petals boldly and irregularly splashed with vermilion red. Its open flowers backlit by warm spring sunshine can turn a bed into a glowing spectacle, but the nearer one gets to it the more garish the display turns out to be – the very opposite of what I want to achieve in my own small garden. The good thing to say about 'Flair', however, is that it has recently produced two excellent pure red sports, 'Red Paradise' and 'Red Revival', which represent an important addition to the colour range in the Single Early Group.

For the sake of completeness, it is worth mentioning other good reliable tulips in this group that are of value in their early season and may be necessary for extending a colour theme across the tulip flowering season. The popular cut flower 'Christmas Marvel' is a strong deep pink; its sport 'Christmas Dream' is paler; and the two might be mixed to good effect. Another sport, 'Merry Christmas', is similar, but with brighter cherry red flowers. Other worthwhile sports are 'White Marvel' and the double-flowered 'Queen of Marvel'. 'Diana' is the best white in this class and the slightly later-flowering 'Yokohama' is a good pure yellow that was once regarded as a Single Early tulip but is now officially classified as a Triumph.

Personally, I don't grow many Single Early tulips, but within the group there are some delightful flowers that I would never be

'Generaal de Wet'

'Keizerskroon'

'Merry Christmas'

'Prins Carnaval' with 'Generaal de Wet' and 'Prince of Austria'

'Van der Neer'

without. 'Apricot Beauty' is commercially successful as a cut flower on account of its special colour, but some of the older varieties described here will stay in production only if we gardeners continue to buy them. 'Prince of Austria' and its sports should be on every gardener's wish list.

'MONSELLA'

Double Early Group tulips

With twice the number of petals than normal, Double Early tulips seem to have been designed to bring a bold splash of colour to their surroundings. 'Monsella', registered in 1981, represents the best of the newer generation of double tulips. Crucially, its flower stems are strong enough to support the heavy flowers, which can open 4 inches/10 centimetres wide in strong sunlight. The petals are broad with rounded tips in a fresh tint of canary yellow on the outside that is a shade darker on the inside. Bright red feathering appears on both sides of each petal. This is often reduced to a single narrow stripe, with no two flowers being exactly the same. The overall effect is bright and sparkling; add to this its sweet lemon fragrance and you have a deservedly popular tulip.

Double Early tulips raise divergent opinions amongst gardeners on the one hand, and between gardeners and bulb growers on the other. The problem is that for many the whole magic of a tulip flower is its simplicity and purity of form, and by doubling the number of petals these are completely lost. I have to agree with this, but it does not mean that I am not prepared to grow them, but rather that I see

them in quite a different way and use them accordingly. The splash of colour they can bring so early in the year is very welcome and their large flowers mean that fewer bulbs are needed to create a bold effect. The same holds true in the vase, making Double Early tulips very popular as cut flowers. This explains their popularity with bulb growers, with some 12 per cent of all tulips grown in the Netherlands today falling into this category. The majority of these, including 'Monsella', are members of a group of sports derived from 'Monte Carlo', a sulphur yellow cultivar first registered in 1955.

The majority of cultivars are around 12 inches/30 centimetres tall, with some being taller and consequently more useful as cut flowers and a few such as 'Yellow Baby' being just 6 inches/15 centimetres tall. Bunched together they make a frothy colourful bouquet and this is also the best way to use them outside, in my opinion. I like to place them on a patio or beside a front door, generously filling containers either on their own or in contrasting associations with taller-growing single tulips or simple foliage plants. So long as they are in a sheltered position, their colourful display will often last for some

LEFT AND ABOVE
'Monsella'

'Carlton'

'Monte Carlo'

Mixed 'Murillo' sports

ABOVE 'Murillo' BELOW 'Oranje Nassau' and 'Cardinal Mindszenty'

ABOVE 'Oranje Nassau' BELOW 'Peach Blossom'

three weeks, whereupon they can be replaced by something else that is just coming into flower, such as Double Late tulips perhaps.

I have never wanted to grow Double Early tulips in my garden borders as I find their flowers too complicated and fussy for the simplicity that seems to typify the early spring season. Were they to flower in early summer along with peonies, roses and irises they would look at home, but amidst my species *Narcissus*, low-growing *Scilla siberica* and simple Single Early Group tulips their scale is just too gross. However, I have admired their use in public parks when planted in wide drifts of a single colour. In particular the repeated pools of orange created by hundreds of 'Oranje Nassau' spread across the undulating landscape of the Keukenhof one year were truly dramatic. They would not have looked as good in my small, enclosed back garden. However, it is worth noting that the success of this scheme relied purely on the massing of colour and not on the individual beauty of the flowers themselves.

Double Early tulips were first recorded early in the seventeenth century with multiple sets of petals per flower. As they were top heavy and susceptible to wind damage, their popularity did not take off until the introduction of the cultivar 'Murillo' by Gerard Leembruggen in 1860. Since then 'Murillo' and its sports have expanded into a group of more than 160 cultivars in a wide range of colours from white ('Schoonoord'), yellow ('Mr van der Hoef'), orange ('Oranje Nassau') and bright pink ('Peach Blossom') to the rich dark tones of the violet purple of 'David Teniers', to name just some of the most popular. Being interrelated, they display a remarkable degree of uniformity in terms of height and flowering time. This leads bulb catalogues to offer one of the most appalling colour mixtures available to us gardeners from any group of plants I can think of. Great rivers of these dolly mixture offerings are a notorious feature at the Keukenhof garden each year. Maybe in the context of celebration they can serve to lighten our spirits, as might the bravado of the fair, but this should surely remain the only place we would ever wish to encounter them.

Today, production in the Netherlands is dominated by 'Monte Carlo' and its many sports, including 'Monsella'. The two cultivars are quite similar, but 'Monte Carlo' is predominantly sulphur yellow with only very faint red feathering on the petals, while 'Monsella' is dramatically feathered red and a noticeably paler shade of yellow. Other notable sports include 'Abba', a glowing tomato red, and 'Viking', which is orange red with a yellow base. Both can exhibit slight yellow flaming and like their parent perform extremely well outside.

Recent introductions have focused on cultivars suitable for forcing and with longer stems for the vase. One of these, 'Verona', was registered in 1991. It is 16 inches/ 40 centimetres tall with fresh primrose yellow flowers that are occasionally streaked green on the outside. Unfortunately, it is susceptible to fungal diseases as a garden tulip and where this pale tint is called for a better choice would be 'Montreux', which was registered in 1990. The colour is a very pale creamy yellow, the base is yellow and as the flowers mature they develop a pinkish red glow on the outside. I have never grown these, but could imagine combining them with drifts of *Euphorbia amygdaloides* var. *robbiae*, which would be covered with clouds of chartreuse blooms at the same time that these cultivars were in flower.

Finally, we must not forget 'Fringed Beauty', officially classified as a Fringed Group tulip which arose as a sport of an old Double Early tulip, and still often listed with them in bulb catalogues. It has bright red flowers with boldly fringed petals that are highlighted in rich glowing yellow. This is one of the few doubles I have grown and enjoyed. The plants are short, growing only 10 inches/25 centimetres high, but have a neat and tidy appearance that makes them ideal in more formal situations lining paths and borders.

At the end of the day, gardeners must decide for themselves what to grow. I do not think I will be dipping any further into this group even though I can see why they appeal to others. As pot plants and cut flowers they have their uses and this is how I shall continue to enjoy them.

'DAYDREAM'

Darwinhybrid Group tulips

This Darwinhybrid tulip has one characteristic that sets it apart from all other members of the group. 'Daydream', registered in 1980, arose as a sport of 'Yellow Dover' and when the buttercup yellow flowers first open it is hard to tell it from its parent. However, by the second morning its flower colour has begun to darken and gradually over the next few days the flowers become a warm glowing medley of light toffee orange. This transition never ceases to enthral me, as the tulip's personality seems to move from fresh impishness to seductive maturity.

The colour when fully developed calls out for company; it can be contrasted with bright blues and purples as might be provided by hyacinths, grape hyacinths (*Muscari armeniacum*) and Triumph tulips such as 'Negrita' or 'Passionale'. Alternatively, it can be added to a rich mixture of other warm-tinted tulips such as the mahogany brown Triumphs 'Abu Hassan' and 'Gavota' or the redder 'Jan Reus', and of course 'Black Parrot' and 'Queen of Night' could be used to increase the gravitas.

Like all Darwinhybrid tulips, 'Daydream' has very large flowers which open out widely in sunshine. Its scale allows me to use it as a dot plant repeating through a border of pale green foliage and fresh yellow euphorbia flowers. Likewise it can be used to accent a planting of the similarly creamy yellow Viridiflora tulip 'Spring Green'.

Darwinhybrids are monster tulips, sometimes with blooms bigger than a man's hand. In many ways they represent the best and the worst achievements of the tulip breeders. For many years I could not imagine why anyone would want to grow such gross tulips in their gardens. With their huge blooms held atop thick 24 inch/60 centimetre tall stems, their scale seems far more appropriate for public green spaces than the intimate confines of a private garden. Indeed, public parks, traffic islands and shopping malls are the places where most of us have encountered them. My conversion came about with the discovery that these strong vigorous tulips are reliably perennial in the garden without needing to be lifted each year, and that as a consequence of this mistreatment the flowers they produce are significantly smaller than those of newly planted bulbs. In parks, the flower beds are replanted each year to produce their eyecatching displays. In my own

'American Dream'

'Apeldoorn'

'Apricot Impression'

'Banja Luka'

'Diplomate'

garden, 'Daydream' reappears every year, growing no more than 20 inches/50 centimetres tall with flowers that bring contrasts with their surroundings by virtue of their open form and colour more than with an inappropriate scale. A new and exciting sport of 'Daydream' is now available. 'American Dream' has a red-edged flower that becomes flushed warm russet orange when mature; needless to say this is top of my wish list of new cultivars to grow.

It was in the 1940s that Dirk Lefeber had the idea of crossing the then popular strong late-flowering Darwin tulips with his selection of the rich red, earlier-flowering *Tulipa fosteriana* – 'Madame Lefeber'. The idea was to combine the sturdy Darwins with the bold flowers of the Fosteriana to create a mid-season-flowering tulip that would be suitable for outdoor bedding. The Darwinhybrids that resulted lived up to these expectations and have become universally popular. The earliest to be registered were all red, but subsequently orange, yellow and even pink entered the colour range. Of these early introductions 'Oxford' (1945), orange scarlet with a bold yellow base, is outstanding and probably the best of the reds for use in the garden. 'Parade' and 'Apeldoorn' are two more reds that were registered in 1951 and remain extremely popular to this day. All have subsequently produced yellow sports and forms suffused with and streaked in orange and red such as 'Golden Oxford', 'Golden Apeldoorn', 'Oxford Elite', 'Apeldoorn Elite', 'Blushing Apeldoorn', 'Orange Queen' and even fringed forms such as 'Fringed Apeldoorn' and 'Fringed Solstice'.

'Hollands Glorie' came from crossing the old red Darwin 'Bartigon' with the Fosteriana 'Madame Lefeber'. Its huge red flowers deepen in tone as they age. A later addition to the reds arose from a similar cross that had produced 'Apeldoorn'; it was registered as 'Diplomate' in 1950. Flowering later than most other Darwinhybrids and only 20 inches/ 50 centimetres tall, 'Diplomate' can be a useful cultivar for bridging the mid and late tulip seasons.

'Gudoshnik'

'Lighting Sun'

The first non-red Darwinhybrid to be introduced was 'Oranjezon' in 1947, resulting from a cross between the Single Early tulip 'Generaal de Wet' and a Greigii tulip. Initially this was classified as a Triumph tulip, but its character is typical of the Darwinhybrids. Its bold, perfectly rounded flowers are a pure strong orange, probably the clearest orange in the whole tulip assortment. It grows 20–24 inches/50–60 centimetres tall.

The first non-red cultivar to be actually classified as a Darwinhybrid, 'Gudoshnik', is another of my favourites. It was registered in 1952, the year I was born, and, like me, it is still going strong and quite unpredictable. The large rounded flowers have a pale yellow base colour which is streaked and splashed with orange and red. Every flower is different; some are almost pure yellow while others are heavily marked.

'Gudoshnik' is a subtle blend of apricot tints that can be contrasted with bolder colours such as the rich purple provided by the Triumph tulip 'Negrita' or the darker-toned *Hyacinthus orientalis* 'Woodstock'. Most Darwinhybrids are, however, far more stridently coloured and less easily used in a small garden. 'Ad Rem' is orange scarlet edged with yellow; 'World's Favourite' is red edged with brilliant yellow; and for sheer

'Ollioules'

'Oxford' and 'Yellow Oxford'

'Parade' and 'Golden Parade'

spectacle nothing can outshine 'Banja Luka', a new sport from 'Apeldoorn', with its scarlet red flowers heavily streaked in vivid yellow.

While the Darwinhybrid Group is dominated by orange, red and yellow flowers, there are others to be aware of which might come in useful when planning mid-season colour schemes. 'Elizabeth Arden' is an old dark salmon pink cultivar that has almost disappeared from production. In its place, brighter, brick red or salmon 'Van Eijk' is rapidly gaining popularity. Alternatively the more sophisticated 'Ollioules' is an unusual colour of pale pink that fades to pure white towards the edges of its petals.

Other colours are to be found in a group of large and unusually early-flowering cultivars. 'Pink Impression' was the first of these to be registered in 1979, having been raised from a cross between a red Triumph tulip called 'Eurovisie' and the breeder's favourite, the Fosteriana tulip 'Madame Lefeber'. Its sports all flower at the same time, some ten days earlier than most other Darwinhybrids: 'Apricot Impression' is light orange, 'Red Impression' is mid-toned red, 'Salmon Impression' is soft pink and the most recent addition, 'Design Impression', is dark pink with variegated foliage.

There are no white Darwinhybrids, and in a planting scheme calling for it the best option would be the creamy white Fosteriana tulip 'Purissima' or the Single Late marble white 'Maureen'. The nearest to white we can come to here is with 'Ivory Floradale', which is in reality a very pale yellow. This extremely attractive cultivar is deservedly popular and could be used in combinations with other yellow tulips, adding contrasts by way of height and the size of its flowers.

In the first year after planting the bulbs, the flowers are best cut for the vase, with the knowledge that their subsequent return will be as smaller blooms more in scale with our private gardens. For a bold splash of colour in the middle of spring, there is nothing to rival a bed of Darwinhybrids. A border at the heart of my garden filled with 'Gudoshnik' and contrasted with nearby patches of purple 'Negrita' becomes its focal point for three weeks every spring without any effort on my behalf – a good reminder that tulips need not be high maintenance when you choose the right sorts.

'Pink Impression'

'Van Eijk'

'World's Favourite'

'NEGRITA'

Triumph Group tulips

This classic Triumph tulip has been the starting point of many planting schemes in my own garden over many years. Like certain other plants that we value for their reliability and positive contribution to our gardens, 'Negrita' is truly indispensable. It comes into flower in the middle of the tulip season, about a week later than the Darwinhybrids and conveniently overlapping with them. Its flowers are slightly larger than many of the other Triumphs; they are a blend of rich bright purples with blue basal blotches edged yellowish white on the inside. It is some 18 inches/45 centimetres tall when it first comes into flower, but by the end of its long display, some three weeks later, it has usually grown to nearly 26 inches/ 65 centimetres, with thick sturdy stems that have no problems in supporting the flowers.

A strong clear colour such as this can be used to make bold contrasts with many other flowers and bulbs in the midst of the spring garden. Its stature is sufficient to allow it to be mixed with bright yellow and orange Darwinhybrids for a truly show-stopping display. It can also be used with other Triumph tulips or members of other groups such as the Lily-flowered, Fringed and

Single Late tulips, all of which contain cultivars with bold clear colours for contrasting effects. However, one combination I came across of 'Negrita' with the pure white Triumph tulip 'White Dream' was harsh, with too much contrast for my taste, but this is always a subjective matter.

Triumph tulips are undoubtedly the most important group in today's market and in the Netherlands around 45 per cent of tulip acreage is assigned for their production. They were created by crossing Single Early tulips with mid- and late-flowering tulips, with the deliberate intention of creating uniform mid-season cultivars suitable for mass bedding which would also be useful for forcing as cut flowers. The breeding programmes started some hundred years ago and continue to the present day, with each year seeing the introduction of new and interesting coloured forms. The emphasis today is very much on the production of better cultivars for the cut flower trade and, unfortunately, only a very small proportion of these are ever made available for gardeners to try, even though many would grow happily outside.

LEFT 'Synaeda Blue' and 'Negrita'

ABOVE 'Negrita'

Triumph tulips grow to around 20 inches/50 centimetres tall with sturdy stems and a single egg-shaped flower that are able to withstand the worst of the spring weather. Their mid-season flowering makes them the standard tulip for garden bedding schemes and the colour range is enormous. Importantly, purple, violet and mauve shades are very well represented in this group, in contrast particularly with the other mid-season tulips, the Darwinhybrids, which are mainly red, orange and yellow. Not only are there single-coloured flowers in all tints and shades imaginable, but also many cultivars have bicoloured or multi-coloured flowers which make them increasingly desirable as cut flowers to be examined at close quarters. To begin to list these here could turn this section into a tedious list when really the colour variations are so subtle that the plants have to be seen to be fully appreciated. However, some cultivars such as 'Negrita' deserve our attention and can form the bases for evaluating and identifying variations and improvements in the assortment as a whole.

'Negrita' is the classic purple Triumph tulip, and other cultivars that are freely available to make harmonious mixtures and associations with it are 'Attila', a light violet purple; 'Barcelona', light purple; and slightly pinker than 'Attila', 'Don Quichotte', violet pink; 'Passionale', with violet purple outside and a beetroot purple interior; 'Purple Prince', shorter growing with mid-purple flowers; and 'Hans Anrud', deep purple with distinctive black stems.

The bicoloured Triumphs are best used alone rather than mixed with other tulips. Two well worth growing in this colour range are 'Arabian Mystery', a deep purple with prominent white petal margins, and 'Synaeda Blue', a taller-growing and more intensely coloured flower. 'Arabian Mystery' is widely available and at only 16 inches/40 centimetres tall is best used in a prominent position on the corner of a flower border. 'Synaeda Blue' is up to 26 inches/65 centimetres tall and may be less sturdy in the open garden. Unfortunately, I cannot write from experience as I have yet to find it being offered for sale, but when it is, I shall not miss the opportunity to grow this beautiful tulip. The flowers are intense violet purple which fade to white at their margins and when open reveal a glowing yellow base haloed in white.

'Shirley' is distinctive; its ivory white petals are finely edged in purple with small spots and streaks also appearing lower down as well as on the white base of its flowers. It mixes well with similar plain-coloured varieties, but on its own tends to look washed out and weak.

The colour of a tulip is not always simple to describe, as often it is the result of different pigments superimposed upon one another in streaked and feathered patterns. What I might consider violet or mauve others might see as pink, and these opinions might vary depending upon the type and angle of light falling on a particular flower. 'Beau Monde' is a case in point. The ivory white flowers have a broad, delicately tinted outer flame which I would call violet purple, but which is officially rhodonite red, the colour of a pink mineral. This cultivar has large flowers in scale with its 26 inches/65 centimetres height and is often placed in the Darwinhybrid group by mistake. At 20 inches/50 centimetres tall, 'Rosario' is a more typical Triumph with clear pink-tinted flowers and a prominent white base. In comparison, 'Meissner Porzellan' is more complex, its white flowers being prominently edged and streaked in shades of warm pink.

With 'Peer Gynt' and 'Leo Visser' we have much stronger tints of pink to play with, but for dramatic impact 'Blenda' is an intense dark rose hue with a prominent white base. These exciting flowers seem to radiate energy when lit from behind. 'Page Polka' is similar and could be substituted for it or included in a mixture of these complementary tints.

'Garden Party' has crisp white flowers edged in carmine red to give a bold pink impact. Personally I prefer the more delicate effect of 'New Design', which is a pale yellow flower fading to light pink towards the petal edges. As these flowers age the pink tone intensifies and when they are fully open a delicate yellow base is revealed. Unusually, 'New Design' has

'Attila'

'Annie Schilder'

'Barcelona'

'Arabian Mystery'

'Bastogne'

'Beau Monde'

'Blenda'

'Blue Champion'

ABOVE 'Calgary' BELOW 'Garden Party'

ABOVE 'Couleur Cardinal' BELOW 'Gavota' with 'Warsawa'

ABOVE 'Don Quichotte' BELOW 'Golden Melody'

'Hollandia'

'Ile de France'

'Jan Reus'

'Negrita' and 'Shirley'

'Lydia'

ABOVE 'Makassar' BELOW 'Montevideo'

ABOVE 'Mary Housley' BELOW 'New Design'

ABOVE 'Meissner Porzellan' BELOW 'Orange Cassini'

variegated margins to its broad leaves that begin pink and fade with time to white.

There are many red Triumph tulips to choose from. Strong clear reds that I will not attempt to differentiate in words are 'Charles', 'Friso', 'Hollandia', 'Ile de France', 'Oscar', 'Sevilla' and 'Red Present'. More complex is 'Bastogne', which has dark red informal flowers that in certain lights seem to have a hint of toffee orange about them. It grows 24 inches/60 centimetres tall and makes an excellent back-of-border cultivar. 'Cassini' is a more typical Triumph, growing 18 inches/45 centimetres tall with brownish red flowers; its sport 'Orange Cassini' is more dramatic. The two together make a sumptuous mixture.

The darkest red of all is 'Jan Reus', an almost black crimson flower that is ideal for bringing contrast and drama to white, pink or purple colour schemes. I would not be without it.

'Couleur Cardinal' is another classic tulip popular with collectors. It used to be considered a Single Early tulip and its relatively short stature at around 15 inches/35 centimetres seems to confirm this, but it flowers later and therefore fits better with the mid-season-flowering Triumphs. Its true date of introduction is unknown, but it was first described in 1845. Clearly this is a tough little tulip and its colour is magical. Inside, the petals are scarlet red, which on the outside is overlaid by a broad purple flame. In strong light the flowers acquire a complex iridescence that suggests they would glow in the dark, but of course that would make them even more unique than they already are. Their sweet fragrance is yet another facet of their flowers to be appreciated. 'Couleur Cardinal' has produced a small number of sports, all of which are highly prized: 'Arma' is a fringed form of its parent, 'Rococo' is a dark mysterious parrot, and probably the most important of all is 'Prinses Irene', which has a rich orange flower with a complex outer purple flame.

'Prinses Irene' is my first thought if I am thinking about orange-flowered Triumphs or

'Oscar'   'Page Polka'   'Passionale'

indeed orange-flowered tulips in general. The beautiful flowers are both effective from a distance as well as being captivating at close quarters. Since its introduction in 1949 it has, in its turn, produced a number of splendid sports: 'Fire Queen', a richer orange with the added bonus of a cream variegated edge to the leaves; 'Hermitage', tangerine red; the Double Late 'Orange Princess', a pinker orange; and 'Prinses Margriet', yellow with the purple flame. All could be mixed together to create a mixture of harmonious tints, but frustratingly most are only made available to cut flower growers.

Another orange tulip that is sometimes in flower before many Single Early tulips, yet is classified as a Triumph, is 'Orange Monarch'. It is 18 inches/45 centimetres tall with irregular rounded flowers of rich mahogany red edged with orange. In years that it comes into flower early, it seems to stay in bloom for more than three weeks.

Orange is not the most common colour in the Triumph assortment, but when a Darwinhybrid would be too gross, they are worth seeking out. The following cultivars are produced mainly for cut flower growers, but that does not mean we should not ask our bulb suppliers for them, as supply would surely follow demand. 'Annie Schilder' is deep orange with lighter edges to the petals and dark-coloured stems. It makes a good alternative to the Single Late tulip 'Dillenburg', albeit earlier flowering. 'High Society' is similar with larger flowers and 'Mary Housley' is paler, apricot shaded with finer smaller flowers. Bold and radiant, 'Prins Claus' has larger flowers

resembling a small Darwinhybrid, a clear orange with a pale creamy yellow outer flame.

'Montevideo' is especially striking. The flowers start off pale yellow and as they age, orange streaking gradually increases down from the edges of the petal to eventually dominate. These bold patterns do not quite reach their bases, which continue to glow yellow.

Yellow Triumphs are similarly useful. Probably the best known are 'Golden Melody' and the lighter 'Yellow Present'. My favourite is 'Makassar', which is deep canary yellow and noticeably later flowering than the rest. Once more this tulip is falling out of production, but its place is being filled by two new and vigorous cultivars, 'Strong Gold' and 'Yellow Flight'. I have yet to grow these two newcomers, but all the indications are that they are excellent garden forms. When a taller variety is called for 'Jan van Nes' at 24 inches/60 centimetres tall is a useful alternative, and when more complex colouration is desirable 'Fortissimo' is pleasing, with pale yellow petals flamed in darker shades of buttercup yellow.

White-flowered tulips are indispensable. They can be used in almost any associations in the garden as well as being useful in mixtures with other coloured tulips. 'White Dream' is the cultivar most bulb catalogues offer and deservedly so. It is 20 inches/50 centimetres tall with ivory white flowers and yellow anthers and stands up well in the open garden. My only reservation about this variety is that it did not return reliably in my garden whereas 'Pax' comes back year after year without being lifted for the summer months. 'Pax' is slightly shorter

'Pax'

'Prinses Irene'

'Rosario'

'Shirley'

'Synaeda Blue'

'White Dream'

and the flowers are pure white. Its flowering period is incredibly long and in a good year, they can remain effective for nearly a month.

A new white only registered in 1995 has already gained an Award of Garden Merit from the Royal Horticultural Society. 'Calgary' is only 8 inches/20 centimetres tall with relatively large square flowers. The colour is ivory white with a broad pale yellow flame on the outermost petals. The flame quickly fades to ivory white, while the flowers remain effective for weeks on end no matter what the weather throws at them. Its stocky habit lacks the slim grace of more typical Triumph tulips, but it is ideal for mass bedding or could be effective as an understorey to taller-growing varieties.

The bicoloured Triumphs are often very striking and make excellent cut flowers. The darker-coloured varieties can work well in associations with other tulips, but the most brightly coloured forms are best treated as stand-alone specimen groups in the open garden. 'Abu Hassan' is cardinal red with a yellow margin; 'Gavota', with darker maroon red petals also with a yellow margin, is similar and ideal for associating with other yellow and orange tulips.

Oozing sophistication and style, 'Slim Whitman' has dark brown red flowers with crisp golden yellow edges and dark green, wavy leaves with golden yellow margins. Never have I seen such a formal-looking plant. 'Helmar' is less subtle, with primrose yellow flowers heavily flamed with ruby red. However, the most outstanding varieties bear gleaming white flowers with rich red flames and feathering. 'Happy Generation' is ivory white with dark red flames while 'Zurel' is more heavily stained with a beetroot purple feather.

Already this is a long list and it could go on and on. The key is to decide upon the colour scheme you want and then track down appropriate cultivars. The danger is that you buy in too many different colours and end up with a disorganized mixture.

'MRS JOHN T. SCHEEPERS'

Single Late Group tulips

A tulip standing 24 inches/60 centimetres tall with a flower as big as a man's hand will have an impact upon its surroundings, especially when, as in the case of 'Mrs John T. Scheepers', they are bright yellow. This giant tulip's history and date of introduction are unknown, but it was first recorded as the winner of an Award of Merit from the KAVB in 1930 and one year later it received a First Class Certificate.

Its size and vigour seem to derive from the fact that it possesses double the normal number of chromosomes, making it what is referred to by geneticists as a tetraploid. Most tulips have twenty-four chromosomes, which during cell division associated with sexual reproduction align themselves into twelve pairs that are pulled apart to form egg and pollen cells with just twelve single chromosomes each. The number of chromosomes in such special cells is called the haploid number, and is constant for any species of plant or animal. In the case of a tulip it is written as $n = 12$. Following sexual union the egg and pollen cells fuse and the normal chromosome number is restored. This is referred to as the diploid number for the species, and in the tulip's case this is written as $2n = 24$.

However, in the case of 'Mrs John T. Scheepers' its forty-eight chromosomes indicate that at some point in its history two cells with the full complement of chromosomes succeeded in uniting to produce a new individual with double the number of chromosomes: a tetraploid. This phenomenon occurs in many plant families and usually results in considerably larger plants and, often, reduced fertility. In some cases sexual reproduction remains possible and when this occurs, for example with the original diploid form of the plant, a triploid may arise with three times the haploid number of chromosomes for the species. Polyploidy is therefore a useful tool in understanding the relationships between plant species and their cultivars.

'Mrs John T. Scheepers' has forty-eight chromosomes and it has been used in breeding programmes to create equally vigorous cultivars which are triploid with thirty-six chromosomes. Of these, 'Maureen' is an outstanding bold white cultivar, indispensable in the late season, and 'Renown' is a pink cultivar that has gone on to produce numerous coloured sports that tend to dominate the Single Late Group assortment to this day. 'Maureen' and all the sports of

'Atlantis'

'Bleu Aimable'

'Big Smile'

'Blushing Lady'

'Dillenburg'

'Renown' are grown outdoors in warmer climates as an important cut flower crop. These are tolerant of heat and resist sun scorch, but in order for them to be grown in areas of the world such as southern Italy, the south of France and parts of America and Australia they need to be subjected to an artificial cold treatment, the so-called 5°C treatment, before being planted out.

It is not as easy to give a simple overall description of the Single Late Group as it is with most of the other tulip groups. The group has been assembled over the years from tulips with mixed and varied backgrounds that only had in common the fact that they flower very late in the tulip season; in the Netherlands this means they begin to flower around the end of April and throughout May. Over the years the group has been used to gather together the leftovers from different groups that no longer justify separate treatment within the official classification. Nowadays it embraces the old Dutch and English Cottage tulips, Darwins and breeders; however, late-flowering cultivars with common distinctive characteristics such as the late-flowering doubles, Fringed, Lily-flowered and Viridiflora forms have been extracted and put into their own groups. In general, what we are left with here is late-flowering, long-stemmed, single and multi-flowered tulips. Few of these are of interest to the producers of cut flowers with

the already noted exceptions of 'Maureen' and the 'Renown' sports, as they take longer to come into flower than the ubiquitous Triumph tulips, for example. However, for gardeners this group is a rich source of exceptional cultivars.

The massive flowers and stature of 'Mrs John T. Scheepers' and her offspring at first sight seem quite out of scale with most people's private gardens. This is especially so when we encounter them being used in massed bedding displays in public gardens. However, these very qualities render them extremely useful when used in mixed or herbaceous borders. When flowering in late spring, their companions will be growing rapidly and all too easily overwhelm shorter and smaller-flowered tulip cultivars. I would never recommend planting a specimen group of these giants, but rather suggest that they be used randomly and sparsely across whole borders or even sections of a garden. In this way, they can fill the canvas with colour for a few weeks before early-summer flowers take over the display. Their vigour is such that they will not need lifting for summer storage, which would be impractical in such situations anyway. I use 'Mrs John T. Scheepers' across the back of a border where bold clumps of *Eupatorium purpureum*, *Aster umbellatus* and *Miscanthus sinensis* grow. These are all high-summer performers that start into growth relatively late in the year. In spring they

'Dreamland'

'Grand Style'

'Greuze'

are simply green and the tulips turn the area into something worth looking at. The slow start into growth of these perennials has the advantage that the tulip's leaves are not submerged under their neighbours' foliage and have enough time to bask in the sunshine and build up strength for next year's display.

When 'Mrs John T. Scheepers' is not being offered for sale, almost certainly 'Big Smile' will be. This is just as impressive as its parent. It arose by crossing 'Mrs John T. Scheepers' with *Tulipa eichleri* 'Excelsa'. The tall oval-shaped flowers are lemon yellow on opening, maturing to deeper yellow during its long flowering period. 'Kingsblood' is also part of the family, with flowers the same shade of deep red to be found in the Lily-flowered tulip 'Red Shine'. Unlike the rest of its kin, the flowers are of a more modest size which might suit certain situations better.

'Renown', which I have already named as the most important cultivar in the 'Mrs John T. Scheepers' family, is a triploid tulip which has soft red flowers that are paler at the edges and a yellow base edged with blue. The flowers are very large, as indeed are its bulbs, and it grows to 26 inches/65 centimetres tall. Its most important sports are 'Avignon', orange pink, which is particularly attractive in bud when bronze and terracotta shades are developing; 'Cri de Coeur',

primrose yellow with a cherry red flame; 'La Courtine', which has two-tone yellow flowers with long hard red streaks on the outside, ugly beyond compare; 'La Madeleine', pale yellow; 'Roi du Midi', deep yellow; and possibly the most popular of all, 'Menton', a light pink with a faint orange overlay. 'Menton' in its turn has produced a most attractive sport, 'Dordogne', which has a warm orange glow to the otherwise pink blooms.

'Inglescombe Yellow' is another triploid tulip dating from 1906. Today it is only to be found growing in historic collections such as that at the Hortus Bulborum in the Netherlands. This is not such a problem as we have many other yellow tulips to use in its place. Its vigorous characteristics are to be enjoyed in two of its sports: 'Princess Margaret Rose' and 'Vlammenspel'. It also produced the parrot tulip 'Texas Gold', which in turn has sported 'Texas Fire' and 'Texas Flame'.

I am especially fond of 'Princess Margaret Rose'. Registered in 1944, it is only 18 inches/45 centimetres tall with clear yellow flowers heavily streaked from the edges of its petals in reddish orange, each flower being slightly different from the next. With the sun behind them, a clump of these jolly flowers always lifts my spirits. Again, such bicoloured flowers are probably best grown in isolation

'Kingsblood'

'Maureen'

'Queen of Bartigons'

'Menton'

'Recreado'

'Pink Diamond'

'Renown'

'Pink Jewel'

'Sorbet'

'Princess Margaret Rose'

'Zomerschoon'

rather than mixed with too many other colours. 'Vlammenspel', registered in 1941, is a similar yellow with a more concentrated bold red flame on the outside. I find the contrast harsh and far less appealing. Both of these varieties are scarce and disappearing from commercial production.

The blend of yellow and red in 'Princess Margaret Rose' moves us in the direction of orange and by far the most exciting orange tulip, 'Dillenburg'. It is one of the old breeder tulips, first introduced in 1916. Although it grows 24 inches/60 centimetres tall, its flowers are not excessively large. The colour is best described as a medley of orange and terracotta, warm and seductive with the bonus of a sweet fragrance. Regrettably this tulip is nearing extinction in the trade with its place being taken by 'Annie Schilder', an earlier-flowering Triumph of almost identical colouration and far more vigorous.

Pink is represented in the Single Late Group in many different guises and intensities. 'Dreamland', with reddish pink flowers with a wide ivory outer flame and a white base, is one of the most dramatic and effective. Its flowers are of medium size and are held 24 inches/60 centimetres tall. There is some debate as to which is the best pure pink in this group. In England 'Clara Butt', an old variety, is still very popular. But it is not grown in the Netherlands, as from a commercial point of view it grows too slowly. 'Queen of Bartigons' is very similar, still in production but regrettably susceptible to fungal infections. Both, if you can find them, grow 22 inches/55 centimetres tall.

With the more modern and vigorous cultivars 'Pink Diamond', 'Douglas Bader' and 'Pink Jewel' we move progressively from a mid-tone pink to a very pale tint. Again, none of these is large for Single Late Group tulips, all growing 20–22 inches/50–55 centimetres tall. In total contrast, 'Grand Style' is taller and a vivid reddish purple. Personally I like its harsh uncompromising colour and nothing could be better for mixing with all the softer pink shades to inject excitement into your planting schemes.

'Picture'

'Picture' is a tulip like no other, with a flower colour that is neither pink nor mauve. The flowers look as if someone has pinched together its petals to create a small pouch. These charmingly crumpled flowers are not particularly large, but are conveniently held on stems up to 24 inches/60 centimetres tall. Their colour begs to be associated with pinks, purples, violets and mauves. One particularly successful association occurred in my garden when the smoky blue flower spikes of *Camassia leichtlinii* subsp. *suksdorfii* Caerulea Group came into flower near by. 'Picture' is about to lose its unique status, as other pinched-flowered forms have appeared in recent breeding programmes and are in the process of being bulked up for release. It remains to be seen if these, in a range of different colours, will retain the idiosyncratic charm of their predecessor.

White tulips with vivid red feathering never cease to attract attention and seem to be universally popular. We have yet to meet 'Marilyn', the Lily-flowered tulip (see page 122), and 'Carnaval de Nice', the Double Late (see page 140), but here we encounter possibly the most dramatic of all, 'Sorbet'. The large-petalled flowers are soft white, the base is cream and they are vividly streaked with a carmine red flame both inside and out. Growing to over 24 inches/60 centimetres tall, this is a plant that needs using carefully in the garden where it will inevitably dominate all that surrounds it.

In comparison, 'Cordell Hull' is far easier to accommodate even though on paper it might sound very similar. The white flowers are flamed carmine red, with the extent and intensity of these patterns increasing as the flowers mature, eventually becoming almost entirely red. The plants are never more than 22 inches/55 centimetres tall and the flowers are not large, but when lit from behind by late afternoon sun they seem to be on fire. 'Cordell Hull' has produced two attractive sports: 'Montgomery' is white with a fine carmine red rim to the petals, which like its parent becomes broader as the flowers mature; and 'Union Jack' has larger flowers that are white and boldly flamed red with a noticeable blue edge to the white base.

Not surprisingly in such a large and varied group, there are many other bicoloured cultivars that might be encountered in bulb catalogues. One of the best, which is readily

ABOVE 'Picture'

available, is 'World Expression'. The large cup-shaped flowers are very pale yellow, boldly feathered in dark carmine red and held 26 inches/65 centimetres tall. For me the contrast is too harsh, but they are tough reliable garden tulips.

Some of the most beautiful and usable tulips to be found in the Single Late Group are those in the purple violet colour range. 'Greuze', dating from 1891, is a bright, glowing purple with a blue base. The flowers are of medium size and held 22 inches/55 centimetres tall. Production of this desirable cultivar has fallen dramatically in recent times. 'Bleu Aimable' is a paler shade of lilac which is almost blue in soft light. When this plant is not available, this special colour is to be found in the flowers of 'Blue Parrot', its sport. 'Recreado' is a dark deep violet purple with fairly small flowers held 20 inches/50 centimetres tall. 'Cum Laude' is a little taller in a softer shade of dark violet. Obviously all these could be mixed and matched with one another to good effect.

'Atlantis' has a quite different character. The amethyst violet flowers have a broad white edge especially towards the tips of the petals. The flowers are relatively small and noticeably rounded, which is useful for contrasting with other flower shapes in a planting scheme. It grows 22 inches/55 centimetres tall or more and not the 16 inches/40 centimetres that is recorded in the official register of tulip names.

At least one more exceptional tulip needs mentioning here. Its colour would blend perfectly with the purple violet cultivars listed so far. 'Magier' is white with a small violet blue rim to the petals when they first open. As the flowers mature this colour spreads gradually down to eventually turn the whole flower this vibrant hue. It flowers over many weeks with stems some 24 inches/60 centimetres tall, and at every stage its flowers are simply beautiful. Having tempted you, though, I must tell you that this tulip has almost disappeared, but fortunately its place will begin to be assumed in the assortment by the Triumph tulip 'Mata Hari'. This new tulip is taller and later flowering than most Triumph tulips; the colour

'Queen of Night'

is very pale cream with a raspberry edge to the petals with some additional streaking and marking making it very similar to 'Magier'.

Dark tones bring contrast to light-coloured planting schemes and by far the most popular tulip with gardeners for this effect is 'Queen of Night'. The colour is very dark maroon that in soft light looks almost black. It is one of the most reliable tulips in my garden, returning year on year and steadily increasing in number. The small perfectly shaped flowers are held 24 inches/60 centimetres high and it may be used almost anywhere. 'Philippe de Comines' is a slightly more reddish version of 'Queen of Night' with small slim flowers. It makes a delightful change, and where a bolder impact is needed the colour is also to be found in its sport, 'Black Parrot' (see page 135).

Clearly, the Single Late Group has many different faces, and the final set of cultivars I wish to introduce here are further evidence of this. To some gardeners 'Temple of Beauty' and its various sports are the epitome of tulip breeding. These extraordinary tulips have huge elongated flowers on stems easily 30 inches/75

ABOVE 'Queen of Night' and 'Shirley'

'Temple of Beauty'

centimetres tall in a medley of harmonious colours; so why is it that I don't feel the need to grow any of them in my own garden? Well, size isn't everything. These are triploid tulips, which presumably accounts for their stature, and 'Temple of Beauty' arose from a cross involving the salmon rose Lily-flowered tulip 'Mariette', from which it gets its colour and elongated flower shape, and an unknown Greigii cultivar, which has endowed it with faint leaf markings that fade as the plants mature.

'Blushing Beauty' has an apricot yellow flower with a pinkish red outer flame and yellow base. The warm blend of colours is well described in the cultivar name of this sport and it is amongst the most popular of the 'Temple of Beauty' family. 'Blushing Lady' is paler, while 'Perestroyka' is an unusual blend of scarlet red and orange that makes a bold terracotta flower which I must admit I find attractive; but the only sport that I am likely to grow is 'Hocus Poc§us', a two-toned yellow flower with fine yet bold red flaming. I can imagine mixing it with plain yellow 'Big Smile' for a more dramatic effect in one of my garden's flower borders. More sports of 'Temple of Beauty' are soon to be released: 'Deep River' is yellow, and

other names to look out for if these dramatic flowers appeal to you are 'Big Brother', 'El Nino' and 'Long Lady'.

Finally, I need to mention 'Zomerschoon'. This cultivar is still offered for sale today in spite of being one of the oldest cultivars in existence, dating from 1620; not surprisingly the raiser's name is unknown. Its longevity is no doubt accounted for by the fact that it is a triploid. It grows just 16 inches/40 centimetres tall and its relatively large flowers are heavily streaked salmon pink over a pure creamy white ground colour. This is the nearest one can come to the broken tulips of the seventeenth century that were the cause of tulip mania in the Netherlands. Not only is this a very beautiful tulip, but it makes an excellent talking point as well.

ABOVE 'Temple of Beauty'

'COLOUR SPECTACLE'

Multi-flowered tulips

A tulip with more than one flower per plant offers more colour impact than the typical single-flowered varieties, and in some situations this can be a positive advantage. 'Colour Spectacle' produces between two and six single yellow flowers per bulb. The flowers are not large, but with each being boldly streaked scarlet red both inside and outside and deepening in tone as they mature, they certainly live up to their name. 'Colour Spectacle', registered in 1990, is to be found listed as a Single Late tulip and is amongst one of the last of the so-called multi-flowered tulips to flower.

These tulips grow only 20 inches/50 centimetres tall and, like other low-growing, later-flowering tulips, they need carefully placing in the garden in order to prevent them being crowded by nearby perennials. With every bulb producing a small bunch of flowers, some of which will still be in bud while others will be fully open, their overall effect is somewhat untidy. Like the double-flowered tulips that have lost the simple grace of the standard tulip, these multi-flowered varieties are best used massed together to bring wide splashes of colour to garden borders or as additions to container plantings.

From a distance, with low-angled sunlight behind them, a group of 'Colour Spectacle', with its heavily feathered flowers, glows rich orange. This tulip is a sport of the better-known 'Georgette', which is predominantly rich yellow. The edges of each petal are finely rimmed with cerise rose, which can also appear as faint streaking on some of its outer petals as they age. 'Georgette' has produced other sports, most importantly 'Red Georgette', which has pure blood red blooms.

'Antoinette', a more recent introduction, is rapidly gaining admirers. It sits somewhat between 'Georgette' and 'Colour Spectacle', and has pale yellow petals edged with cream that on opening begin to become suffused with pink; this increases and darkens from the edge to eventually overwhelm the whole flower. The delicate medley of pastel tints provides the perfect setting for darker purple- and pink-toned companions. Its steadily changing colour palette has gained it the nickname of the 'Chameleon' tulip, but as we have already seen this is a common characteristic in this group as a whole.

'Candy Club' is yet another multi-flowered tulip that becomes more richly coloured as the

LEFT 'Antoinette' in front of 'Blushing Beauty'

ABOVE Single Late 'Colour Spectacle'

'Colour Spectacle'
(Single Late)

flowers age. The creamy white petals first appear edged and splashed with marks resembling raspberry sauce. These steadily bleed out across its petals to create a mouth-watering treat.

So far, all the multi-flowered tulips described have been members of the Single Late Group. The Triumph Group are earlier flowering and also include some multi-flowered varieties. For sheer impact, 'Orange Bouquet' is impressive. This reliable garden tulip can sometimes be found carrying twelve flowers per plant, their glowing orange red blooms simply saturating the surroundings with colour. Where a darker, purer red is called for, 'Roulette' is a fine choice. Flowering early in the Triumph season and much earlier than 'Red Georgette', 'Roulette' has blood red blooms with a clear yellow base which are neatly organized into individual bouquets of just three to four flowers per plant. These seem to avoid the overcrowded effect typical of most of the other multi-flowering varieties so far described.

At this point, I should also not forget to mention the earlier-flowering Greigii tulip 'Toronto'. It bears three to four flowers per stem. These are a strange shade of red that glows with hints of orange and pink; the base is coloured gold with green. Similar is its soft orange sport 'Orange Toronto', while 'Quebec' is cream with a broad pink outer flame. All grow 15 inches/35 centimetres tall. You should be aware, however, that this multi-flowered characteristic of 'Toronto' and its sports is displayed only when the largest bulbs are planted, and these need to have been stored at high temperatures (25°C) throughout the summer.

The low-growing species *Tulipa praestans* and its cultivars are also multi-flowered. These flower very early in the year when their surroundings are relatively bare. In this respect, it is a far more useful garden tulip than the others described above, all of which could probably be replaced by more elegant, single-flowered tulips of similar colouration in border planting schemes.

'Georgette' (Single Late)

'Orange Bouquet' (Triumph)

'Orange Toronto' (Greigii)

'Roulette' (Triumph)

'Toronto' (Greigii)

Tulipa praestans 'Fusilier' (Miscellaneous)

'RED SHINE'

Lily-flowered Group tulips

The colour of this tulip never ceases to win my admiration, especially when contrasted with the rich green foliage of its companions in my grass border. It begins to flower around the beginning of May and, with clement weather, it will still be effective some three weeks later. Over time the flowers grow larger, opening widely in sunshine to reveal a pure black base.

'Red Shine' is a Lily-flowered tulip with elongated petals that taper to a point at their tips. This feature is perhaps not so pronounced as with some other members of its group, but nevertheless its flowers are both elegant and dramatic. The characteristic shape of the flowers in this group is reminiscent of the elongated tulips so popular in Turkey during the Ottoman Empire. The long tapering petals may curve outwards, as with 'Burgundy' and 'West Point', to produce star-like blooms with refined curvaceous outlines that radiate grace and sophistication.

Lily-flowered tulips are not only elegantly shaped and available in a range of attractive colours, but have earned their popularity with gardeners for two other very important reasons. Firstly, their flowering straddles the end of the mid-season tulip groups and the flowering of most of the late-season tulips, making them extremely useful when planning planting combinations. And secondly, as a group, they are tough and sturdy garden plants, growing strongly and quite easily persuaded to return year on year without their bulbs being lifted for summer storage. Most are fairly tall, between 22–26 inches/55–65 centimetres, which is useful for later-flowering tulips being grown in mixed borders, but there are also some shorter cultivars for use in containers and towards the front of planting schemes.

My personal favourites within the group are the single-coloured cultivars, such as 'Red Shine'. Of these 'Ballerina' is possibly my favourite. Its rich orange toffee flowers are strongly scented, unlike most of the others in its group. Its official description reads like a promotional advertisement: 'Exterior flamed blood red on lemon yellow ground with orange yellow veined edge; inside, feathered marigold orange with capsicum red, buttercup yellow star shaped base, anthers pale golden yellow. Height 55 cm.' I have already written about my combination of its colours and form

LEFT Lily-flowered mixture with pink 'Mariette' centre foreground

ABOVE 'Red Shine'

with that of *Tulipa acuminata* (see page 70). I have also seen it mixed with the similar but darker-coloured Lily-flowered tulip 'Jane Packer' to dramatic effect.

Still at the hot end of the spectrum, 'Aladdin' is only 20 inches/50 centimetres tall with dark scarlet strongly reflexed petals that are crisply edged yellow. It is understandably popular and regularly offered for sale. Its sport 'Aladdin's Record' is even more boldly variegated in primrose yellow. Both are probably best appreciated at close quarters in a container. A flower with more substance, reaching 24 inches/60 centimetres tall and therefore more suitable for the open garden, 'Queen of Sheba' should be on everybody's shopping list. Its broader petals are a dark brownish red, generously edged with a band of rich orange. Such highly decorated blooms need to be given celebrity status and allowed to stand out against a simple harmonious background rather than being mixed and matched with a medley of other tints and hues. Just imagine 'Queen of Sheba' rising above a writhing sea of the bronze form of *Carex comans*.

Purples, mauves and pinks are well represented in the group. The pure deep purple 'Burgundy' cries out to be combined with almost everything else that flowers at the same time. Its deep hue suggests the same contrasting combinations that work for the Single Late tulip deep maroon 'Queen of Night' and the Triumph tulip crimson 'Jan Reus'. With bright yellows such as Lily-flowered 'West Point', the Triumph 'Makassar' or Fringed 'Hamilton' the effect will be electric. However, its purity of colour is possibly best exploited in harmonious schemes with mauve, purple, violet and pink flowers, which are readily available in the late-spring garden, especially from tulips in the Triumph, Fringed and Single Late Groups.

Describing tints and hues of purple in words is not particularly helpful; you really need to see them in real life to appreciate their differences. All of the following would certainly work together in a harmonious mixture. 'Lilac Time' is a pure vibrant violet

purple, lighter in hue than 'Burgundy'. 'Maytime' is a darker reddish violet with a narrow creamy white margin to its petals; when open in sunshine this gives a pleasing variegated effect. More dramatic, 'Ballade', with its magenta purple petals edged with a bold white margin, is spectacular and far more sophisticated in real life than photographs of it might suggest.

The best pink Lily-flowered tulip is undoubtedly 'Jacqueline'. It is 26 inches/65 centimetres tall with impressive deep pink blooms. The shorter-growing (18 inches/45 centimetres) 'China Pink' is also worth growing towards the front of a mixed border, with forget-me-nots (*Myosotis*) as its obvious companion. If you can find it, 'Jan van Zanten's Memory' is spectacular with two-tone pink petals that are palest towards their edges. At 22 inches/55 centimetres tall, it is a versatile plant usable in all garden situations from pots to borders.

'Mariette' is neither pink nor red: officially it is described as deep salmon rose. Its effect in the garden is bold, unlike the gentler pink cultivars so far described, and consequently it is far more difficult to place. Against yellow or orange, it could easily give you nightmares. It has produced a number of sports, the most renowned of which is 'Marilyn'. Its bold white flowers are crisply flamed in deep fuchsia purple, producing one of the most eyecatching blooms of any tulip.

The yellow sport of 'Marilyn' called 'Mona Lisa' is also very popular. Its pale yellow petals are streaked with rich red and when open in sunshine the large flowers are highly attractive. The same flowers when seen as closed buds have a less appealing candy-stripe look which is my personal justification for not growing this cultivar.

Pure bright yellow is available to us with the universally popular cultivar 'West Point'; for its use, see page 157. If its tint is too bright and dominant for you, there are other yellow Lily-flowered tulips to consider. 'Moonshine' is primrose yellow on the outside and somewhat darker yellow inside. The elegantly reflexed

OPPOSITE BOTTOM LEFT Sports of 'Mariette', from back to front: 'Marilyn', 'Macarena' and pink-flamed 'Christina van Kooten', all flowering together with yellow 'Monica' in the foreground

'Aladdin'

'Ballade'

'Ballerina'

'Burgundy'

'Elegant Lady'

'Jacqueline'

'Jan van Zanten's Memory'

'Jane Packer'

'Mariette'

ABOVE 'Marilyn' BELOW 'Maytime'

'Mona Lisa'

'Queen of Sheba'

'Sapporo'

'Red Shine'

'West Point'

'White Triumphator' used with formal precision

petals are not too large and it grows just 20 inches/50 centimetres tall. 'Elegant Lady' is a gentle shade of pale yellow that becomes flushed with pink towards the edges of its petals.

Many other Lily-flowered tulips have been introduced for the cut flower trade and from time to time might be offered to gardeners. 'Sapporo' is one such example which I would like to try as its light yellow flowers progressively fade to white over time. However when a true white tulip is called for there is always one cultivar that should spring to mind, the deservedly popular 'White Triumphator'.

'White Triumphator' has large, elongated blooms on stems that can easily exceed 24 inches/60 centimetres. In spite of its large flowers and height, it resists the worst of the weather and remains effective in the garden for weeks on end. This is definitely a splendid cultivar to round off a survey of the best of the Lily-flowered tulips; but more than this, it stands out as one of the top white-flowered plants available to gardeners in any season.

'White Triumphator' with lower-growing Double Late 'Mount Tacoma'

'BLUE HERON'

Fringed Group tulips

Since 1981 there has been a separate group for the so-called Fringed tulips, which, not surprisingly, have fringed rather than smooth-edged petals. It is a matter of opinion if you think this is an improvement on the normal form of a flower or not. I am fairly ambivalent, as it is only when looking at the flowers close to that the fine ragged edges of the petals are obvious. And indeed, when walking around a garden in which many tulips are growing, it makes a refreshing change to come across a group of Fringed tulips. At their best they always attract attention, and those forms that lend themselves to being forced as cut flowers are extremely popular with flower arrangers.

As to their suitability for the open garden, opinions differ; or more precisely my opinion differs from that of every gardening book and bulb catalogue I have ever read. Many are strong-growing late-flowering tulips capable of making an effective contribution to planting schemes. My reservations come with the way the fine tips of their fringes can all too easily be singed by cold dry winds or burnt and browned by high temperatures and intense sunshine. Many have two-tone flowers with pale fringe tips and these display the problem less prominently than the darker richer-coloured forms such as 'Arma' and 'Burgundy Lace'. This weakness is the first thing I look for when coming across them in a garden and distracts me from appreciating their overall contribution. Also, all eventually begin to fade and, quite naturally, it is the fine tips of the fringe that show the first signs of this.

Reservations aside, I do grow a couple of Fringed tulips and the one that has given me the most pleasure over many years without needing to be lifted is 'Blue Heron'. The colour is a gentle purple fading to a pale lilac near its crystalline fringe. These gentle shades easily blend with plants with blue, violet and deep purple flowers. In my own garden they are woven through a planting of the pure white Lily-flowered tulip 'White Triumphator' and the near black Single Late 'Queen of Night'.

The majority of the Fringed tulips offered today have been produced by hybridizing, but the oldest cultivars arose as natural sports of existing tulips and occasionally such sports occur today. The oldest Fringed tulip still in cultivation is 'Fringed Beauty', which arose as a

LEFT AND ABOVE
'Blue Heron'

'Aleppo'

'Arma'

sport of a very old Double Early tulip called 'Titian'. The multi-petalled flowers are bright red and the bold fringes are highlighted in rich glowing yellow. The plants are short, only growing to 10 inches/25 centimetres tall, and it surprises me how impressive these stocky flowers appear. Like highly decorated military officers, they stand stiffly to attention looking crisp and alert. They make ideal candidates for formal bedding schemes, but offer better value in mixed schemes of perhaps purple or orange tulips in which they introduce points of depth and contrast at a lower height above ground level.

When an existing good garden tulip produces a sport, we can expect it to be similarly tough and reliable. This is the case with the fringed sport of 'Couleur Cardinal', known as 'Arma', registered in 1962. The Darwinhybrids have also produced a number of spectacular fringed sports: 'Fringed Apeldoorn' and 'Fringed Golden Apeldoorn', while 'Fringed Elegance' is a sport of 'Jewel of Spring' and 'Fringed Solstice' is a sport of 'Fringed Apeldoorn'. 'Crystal Beauty', another 'Apeldoorn' sport, is a great improvement on the original 'Fringed Apeldoorn'. Anyone with a camera in their hand will be drawn to these large dramatic blooms.

One of the first hybrids to be introduced in 1959 was the unique white-fringed tulip 'Swan Wings'. When the wine red 'Burgundy Lace' appeared in 1961 it quickly became the most popular in the group. I grow 'Burgundy Lace' in the corner of a herbaceous border filled with drifts of black and white tulips and daffodils: its rich glowing colour is needed to lift the scheme by introducing a bold note of discord. It flowers very late in the season, but, fortunately, being

some 27 inches/70 centimetres tall, it is not swamped by anything growing near by.

Other rich-coloured varieties that perform well in gardens are the glowing orange red 'Noranda', pure red 'Hellas' and 'Red Wing', rich yellow 'Hamilton' and the paler yellow 'Maja'. 'Warbler' has become very popular, for not only does it have bold yellow flowers but its fringe is larger and more noticeable than any of the other single-coloured cultivars.

Today's taste seems to favour the newer hybrids with two-tone flowers, especially when the petal's fringe resembles crystalline sugar. Personally, I find these sickly creations, but they are popular as cut flowers and a vase rather than the garden is definitely the best place for them. If you like this sort of thing, 'Canasta', which is deep red with a pure white fringe, 'Davenport' in pillar-box red with a deep yellow fringe or 'Cummins' in lavender mauve with a white fringe will no doubt appeal. When the colour contrast is gentle, as with 'Fancy Frills', which has an ivory white flame blending into pink at the edges with a lighter rose pink fringe and white base, the result can be acceptable. 'Huis ten Bosch' is a similarly clear pink cultivar, while 'Pink Wizard' is almost white with a gentle tracery of pink that intensifies towards the edges of its fringed petals.

While I tend to favour the more gently coloured members of this group, there is one extraordinarily coloured Fringed tulip that I would like to grow. Called 'Aleppo', it is rich red streaked with pink, with the fringe and base being an indescribable mixture of gleaming apricot and pink. This unique combination is both striking and sophisticated.

'Burgundy Lace'   'Fringed Beauty'

'Fringed Solstice'   'Hamilton'

ABOVE 'Huis ten Bosch' BELOW 'Pink Wizard'   ABOVE 'Noranda' with camassias BELOW 'Swan Wings'

'SPRING GREEN'

Viridiflora Group tulips

If I had to choose just one tulip to grow, 'Spring Green' would be it. It flowers late in the tulip season, by which time the mixed borders in my garden are beginning to fill up. As it grows to only 20 inches/50 centimetres tall, I have to place it carefully to prevent it being overwhelmed by its neighbours. The name 'Spring Green' perfectly captures the spirit of the pleasing flowers. The relatively large-petalled flowers are bright cream shading to yellow with a bold green flame on the outside. They bring freshness and light to their surroundings and easily blend with anything that might be growing near by. I like to use them sprinkled randomly across the whole width of perennial borders to bring interest to the green foliage that tends to predominate this early in the gardening year. All yellows are its perfect companions. The Lily-flowered tulip 'West Point' is slightly taller with a noticeably different-shaped flower. Perennials such as chartreuse-flowered euphorbias, daisy-flowered doronicums and globe-flowered trollius flower early enough to make successful companions, while many different cultivars of *Narcissus* can be used to fill in the background.

Dark-coloured blooms make a bold contrast with this pale-tinted tulip. I particularly like the combination with 'Black Parrot' or its single-flowered parent 'Philippe de Comines'. 'Queen of Night', its double sport 'Black Hero' and even the dark maroon double blooms of 'Uncle Tom' could all be used with equal success.

The green streaks on the outside of the flowers of 'Spring Green' are characteristic of a division of tulips called the Viridiflora Group. These are really tulips for the connoisseur, with intriguing blooms that reward closer inspection. None grows very tall, 'Doll's Minuet' and 'Groenland' being the strongest growing of the group and reaching a height of 22 inches/55 centimetres with proportionally larger flowers. 'Spring Green' comes close at 20 inches/50 centimetres, but most of the rest of the group are sports of a cultivar called 'Artist' and only grow some 12 inches/30 centimetres tall. Use them in discrete clumps towards the front of your borders or grow them for use as cut flowers.

'Artist' was registered in 1947. Its deep salmon pink petals have a wide green flame and the relatively large flowers are held firmly just 12 inches/30 centimetres high above its broad

LEFT AND ABOVE
'Spring Green'

'Adriaan T. Dominique'

'Artist'

'China Town'

'Doll's Minuet'

'Esperanto'

'Golden Artist'

'Groenland'

'Hollywood Star'

plain green leaves. These sturdy garden tulips have returned to flower in my borders without being lifted in the summer, but to safely maintain a collection of these special flowers I should really recommend summer storage.

'Artist' has produced a number of beautiful sports which themselves have also sported to create the dominant look of the Viridiflora Group. 'Golden Artist' is clear yellow occasionally flushed pink with a broad green flame. It is deservedly popular, with a flower colour that is strong enough to allow it to be used in bedding schemes in combination with, for example, low-growing wallflowers in shades of yellow and brown. This sport has itself produced another truly magnificent addition to the assortment. 'China Town' has soft pink petals fading paler to their edges with bold light green flames. Not only are the flowers beautiful but also the leaves are boldly streaked white along their edges to create something quite extraordinary.

'Hollywood' was one of the first 'Artist' sports to be registered in 1956. It is bright red with a dark green flame. In 1987 its own sport, 'Hollywood Star', was registered and this represented an improvement with deeper red-shaded flowers, a moss green flame and leaves bearing a thin yellow-variegated edge. The variegated leaves of 'China Town' were far more impressive when they appeared one year later, but the characteristic had already appeared in the group some ten years early. This was in 1968 with 'Esperanto', another sport of 'Hollywood', and always popular with glowing pink blooms and crisply white-edged leaves.

More recently, in 1993, another variegated-leaved sport of 'Artist' appeared: 'Green River', which has warm apricot-tinted flowers with a light green flame. The foliage is interesting, with wavy-edged leaves bearing a broad band of lemon yellow.

The slightly taller-growing 'Dancing Show' adds the lighter shade of canary yellow to this assortment. It is 18 inches/45 centimetres tall with clear-toned petals with a light green flame on the outside. While this cultivar is less robust than 'Spring Green', it can make a pleasing component of a container planting scheme.

'Violet Bird'

'Yellow Spring Green' and the other taller-growing Viridiflora tulips are the best types for general border planting schemes. This cultivar mixed with its parent makes a magnificent show, but unfortunately it is only infrequently offered for sale to gardeners. Other excellent cultivars include 'Groenland', which has light pink petals fading to white towards their mid-green flame. This in turn has produced the parrot tulip 'Green Wave', which I describe in glowing terms on page 137.

Bolder-hued 'Doll's Minuet' is a particular favourite of mine. The petal shape is similar to that of some Lily-flowered tulips and the green flame is barely visible, but the colour is a radiant purple pink that can bring dramatic contrasts to more gentle-toned planting schemes. 'Eye Catcher' is similarly effective, with brick red flowers that again grow to around 22 inches/55 centimetres tall.

It would be easy to become a collector of Viridiflora tulips, and tulip breeders are

'Yellow Spring Green'

continually searching for new and exciting sports. I have seen many in the trial fields in Holland which I would love to grow but have yet to see offered for sale. Two to be treasured if you ever come across them are 'Adriaan T. Dominique', which is a rich purple pink, paler towards the margins, and the darker violet purple 'Violet Bird', which has a fresh pale green flame.

 'BLACK PARROT'

Parrot Group tulips

Most parrot tulips have arisen as spontaneous mutations of existing tulips with the result that their petals have become enlarged and twisted and in some flowers can be likened to the crossed hooked bills of parrots. Many examples developed huge grotesque blooms that were far too heavy for their stems to carry and, while they could make fascinating cut flowers, they had no use whatsoever in the open garden.

Over the years the very best of these strange flowers have been selected to provide a range of bizarre-shaped blooms on sufficiently sturdy stems. Their colours range from pure white to nearly black and numerous intermediate shades, with many being splashed and streaked in contrasting tones and tints. Some remind me of living sculptures that change every day as their flowers expand and open out. Such extraordinary performances are best seen at close quarters, and Parrot tulips are therefore hugely popular as pot-grown specimens and cut flowers. Only the sturdiest of examples will survive for long in open gardens and all will benefit from a sheltered position out of blustery winds and driving rain.

Although logic tells me that I should not like these misshapen flowers in preference to the refined form of the classic tulip, 'Black Parrot' has become one of my favourite tulips. Its colour, a rich dark maroon, is of course the main reason for this, but unlike many others in the group, its flowers are finely feathered and twisted, not especially large, and held on strong stems no more than 20 inches/50 centimetres tall. Elegant rather than grotesque, 'Black Parrot' makes the perfect dark-shaded tulip to bring contrast into light-toned planting schemes.

Its open cup-shaped flowers with their feather-like petals contrast with the typical egg-shaped form of other single late-flowering tulips; they also draw attention to the pointed petals of Lily-flowered tulips, and they work especially well amongst Viridiflora tulips with their dark-green-streaked flowers. 'Makassar' is a pure yellow, relatively late-flowering Triumph tulip whose flowering period overlaps that of 'Black Parrot'. Combined together in equal numbers these make a dramatic, vividly contrasted spectacle. The equally bold yellow Lily-flowered tulip

LEFT 'Black Parrot' with 'Spring Green'

ABOVE 'Black Parrot'

'Blue Parrot'

'Flaming Parrot'

'Green Wave'

'Moonshine' could serve the same function and may last in flower till later in the season. The bright yellow flowers of the popular Lily-flowered tulip 'West Point' should offer the same dramatic contrast as 'Makassar' and 'Moonshine'; however, its larger flowers open very wide in sunshine and can easily overwhelm the smaller 'Black Parrot'.

Similar dramatic combinations result from combining it with 'Helmar', a rich yellow heavily streaked in dark red; 'Princess Margaret Rose', warm yellow speckled and suffused with orange and red; 'Georgette', a yellow multi-flowered tulip; and its sport 'Colour Spectacle', which is yellow boldly streaked and flamed in red.

A subtler combination results with the creamy yellow Viridiflora tulip 'Spring Green'. 'Black Parrot' can be used either evenly mixed throughout the planting area or alternatively in small groups here and there to add points of contrast that accentuate a dominant 'Spring Green' theme. Flowering equally late in the season, many other Viridiflora tulips make ideal companions. Just two of my favourites are 'Yellow Spring Green' and 'Golden Artist'.

The dark tone of 'Black Parrot' makes it easy to associate with a whole range of other mid- to late-season-flowering tulips, but it is only 20 inches/50 centimetres tall and can be easily overwhelmed by taller-growing varieties. Using it towards the front of a border with taller-growing Lily-flowered tulips behind, such as pale yellow 'Elegant Lady' or deep pink 'Jacqueline', could be very effective, but if these were mixed together the proportions would be wrong. Interestingly though, this difference in height could be exploited in the sort of scheme where a dark-toned carpet of 'Black Parrot' was punctuated by a taller-

'Monarch Parrot'   'Muriel'   'Professor Röntgen'

growing tulip such as 'White Triumphator' or yellow 'Hocus Pocus'.

'Black Parrot' was registered in 1937, having arisen as a sport of 'Philippe de Comines', an old deep maroon Single Late tulip dating from 1891. Its parent is rarely offered for sale today, but the sumptuous colour is readily available in this deservedly popular parrot form. The same is true of 'Bleu Aimable', a highly desirable Single Late tulip that is only occasionally offered for sale. Its unique violet mauve colour, which in soft light can look almost blue, is nowadays readily available in its sport 'Blue Parrot'. While the flowers of 'Bleu Aimable' are quite small, even dainty, which is part of its considerable charm, those of 'Blue Parrot' can become considerably larger. Even so, its flowers are far from being grotesque, with broad wavy petals that become darker toned on the inside around a small white base. 'Blue Parrot' is not a tulip for specimen planting; its crumpled flowers work best as part of a mixed scheme in which it can add its unique colour. It will associate with any purple, mauve, yellow or white tulips flowering around the same time and works especially well amidst clouds of wallflower blossom in more formal bedding schemes.

As for the rest of the Parrot tulips, let personal taste be your guide. In search of new forms, breeders have sometimes exposed bulbs to a form of radiation called roentgen rays. One of the products of this approach is an extremely popular tulip called 'Estella Rijnveld'. The huge flowers are white, overlaid with bold irregular streaks of flaming red. To me this mutant represents the worst of what is possible in the search for novelty, but you might find it spectacular.

Another popular cultivar is the bright yellow streaked red 'Flaming Parrot'. The flowers are usually held wide open atop sturdy 27 inch/70 centimetre tall stems. For a bold splash of colour, nothing else can touch it. This and some others are worth growing occasionally for fun. One in particular that gave me a lot of pleasure is a relatively new cultivar called 'Green Wave'. This sport of the Viridiflora tulip 'Groenland' is a medley of green, white and pink. Its distorted petals twist and writhe in a performance that can last two or three weeks. I grew it in a large pot on my balcony and was fascinated.

Possibly the most important parrot tulip from the cut flower industry's point of view is 'Rococo', a sport of the fabulous 'Couleur Cardinal' and like its parent sweetly scented. Unlike most parrot tulips 'Rococo' is quite short at only 15 inches/35 centimetres. It forces well and flowers mid-season. The flowers are shapely with only the edges of the petals being ruffled and crimped. Like its parent, the deep red blooms are overlaid with purple flames, creating a unique sumptuous richness. Personally, though, I would rather grow single 'Couleur Cardinal' in the garden, but that is not always so easy to find for sale.

'UNCLE TOM'

Double Late Group tulips

Lustrous petals of smouldering deep maroon are crammed into the extravagant blooms of this Double Late tulip, 'Uncle Tom'. For me it is the colour that makes me want to grow this flower, for in no way does this group of tulips ring any of my tulip bells. Here we are entering the same problem area that we encountered with the Double Early tulips. In this case, however, the situation is made worse – or better, depending on your taste – by the fact that their large globular flowers are crammed full of petals and not always tidily. This leads them to be favourably compared with peony flowers, but opinions are divided. My approach is to use them to bring a splash of colour or a contrasting form to planting schemes and try not to think of them as tulips!

Double Late tulips have been known for many centuries and were quite fashionable as curiosities around the end of the seventeenth century. Their bulky flowerheads were often too heavy for their stems and the flowers were notorious for breaking off in wet and windy weather. To some extent the newest cultivars offered to gardeners today have overcome this problem, but they still need to be placed in a sheltered position in the garden, or better still

grown in pots and displayed in a cool greenhouse or conservatory. Although taller than the earlier doubles, most of the cultivars only reach some 20 inches/50 centimetres and therefore are easily overwhelmed by neighbouring perennials in a mixed garden border. Even so, this is probably the best place to grow them outside, as should they be toppled by a storm the damage will be far less obvious than in a more formal bedding scheme.

A bunch of these blooms will amply fill a vase and as cut flowers they all have their admirers. 'Angélique' with its apple-blossom-coloured blooms is universally popular both as a cut flower and with gardeners, who are attracted by seductive close-up photographs of its flowers in bulb catalogues.

Personally, I would never grow Double Late tulips on their own as they simply lack the poise or refinement I expect from a tulip. However, as the supporting cast for classic-shaped tulips they offer the perfect counterpoint. Since they are shorter growing than most late-season tulips they can be used to build a lower plane of colour above which Triumph, Single Late and Lily-flowered tulips can display their elegant

LEFT AND ABOVE
'Uncle Tom'

blooms. Within the assortment, a range of interesting colours exists, as well as many bicoloured cultivars that offer interesting possibilities for creating either contrasting or complementary colour associations.

In spite of being one of the oldest tulips in the present-day assortment, 'Mount Tacoma' (pre 1924) remains possibly the best of its group for use in the garden. With symmetrically shaped pure white flowers on strong stems to 18 inches/45 centimetres high, it tolerates bad weather and can be added to virtually any colour scheme you might have in mind.

'Blue Diamond' is the double sport of the violet purple Triumph tulip 'Prince Charles'. Obviously the two will complement each other perfectly in a planting scheme, but this could be the starting point for a scheme in which other Triumph and Single Late tulips in the purple violet colour range are added: 'Negrita', 'Bleu Aimable', 'Synaeda Blue', 'Cum Laude', 'Greuze' and 'Recreado' are just some of the many possibilities.

'Lilac Perfection' is another gardenworthy double in the similar colour of soft lilac that fades to white towards the centre of its flowers. Again, this is a useful complement for other taller-growing tulips.

An intense deep pink is available in the form of 'Maywonder', a sturdy, weather-resistant flower growing some 20 inches/50 centimetres tall. In comparison, 'Angélique' is far gentler and easier to combine with a range of other hues. This bestselling tulip is a medley of pinks that fade to paler tints towards the petal edges. The effect is reminiscent of apple blossom and makes a perfect foil for darker pink-tinted tulips such as the Triumphs 'New Design' or 'Barcelona' or the splendid Lily-flowered tulips 'Jacqueline' and 'Mariette'. Purples, mauves, violets and also white will also work with this tulip but orange and hard reds should be avoided.

Many Double Late tulips have bicoloured flowers, which make them better suited as cut flowers than as components of garden colour schemes. 'Nizza' is an old cultivar dating from 1939. Its distinctive rounded flowerhead has pale yellow petals heavily streaked and feathered in dark red. 'Golden Nizza' is a more colourful golden yellow sport. Its best-known offspring is 'Carnaval de Nice', a spectacular pure white flower dramatically streaked with dark red. This cultivar, which also displays a white-variegated margin to its leaves, is the only member of this group that justifies specimen treatment in the open garden. A small bed filled with just this one cultivar will win the admiration of all.

A sport of the famous Triumph tulip 'Prinses Irene' is useful when a splash of orange is needed. Like its parent, 'Orange Princess' has bright orange petals with violet purple outer flame markings, but for me the doubling of its petals destroys the magical quality that has kept 'Prinses Irene' in the top ten of garden tulips for more than fifty years.

'Allegretto' is uncompromisingly bold. Its bright rust red petals are generously edged with rich golden yellow. The flowers are large, but held sturdily on 15 inch/35 centimetre stems, giving them the same stocky character I so like in the similarly coloured Double Early tulip 'Fringed Beauty'. The bedding scheme I encountered of 'Allegretto' set amidst a sea of forget-me-nots in London's Kensington Gardens one spring was a revelation. It worked because the tulips were placed randomly and far apart. Each stood proud as a specimen, its substantial flowers floating atop the foaming mass of its tiny companions.

Typical of the sort of doubles that I feel look better in the vase than the garden is 'Wirosa'. Its deep wine red petals are edged with a broad band of creamy white that is best appreciated up close rather than as a distant jumble. Its stems are only 15 inches/35 centimetres tall.

The last Double Late tulip I want to mention is one that I have yet to grow and just hope will turn out to be an equally robust garden variety as its parent. 'Black Hero' is the double sport of 'Queen of Night' with the same rich maroon purple to almost black flowers. Unlike most other tulips in its group, it is tall at some 24 inches/60 centimetres, which suggests all sorts of possibilities within the late-spring mixed border. Its useful height should not be a problem since its flowers are relatively small as well as being a pleasing globular shape.

'Angélique'

'Black Hero'

'Blue Diamond'

'Carnaval de Nice'

ABOVE 'Lilac Perfection' BELOW 'Nizza'

ABOVE 'Mount Tacoma' BELOW 'Orange Princess'

 Tulipa sprengeri

Miscellaneous tulips: mid- to late-flowering species

As with tulip cultivars, there are different species flowering throughout the tulip season, from the very earliest, such as *T. biflora* and *T. polychroma*, to the absolute last, *T. sprengeri*. The more you grow tulips the more irresistible become the species. Even though these are not plants with which to paint your garden with broad sweeps of colour, they are guaranteed to bring considerable satisfaction. On the one hand they bring you closer to the tulip's origins and history, and on the other they exhibit a refinement and purity missing from some of the more dramatic modern cultivars.

The species most suitable for the open garden will have either to have bold flowers held high enough to be visible from afar or to be sufficiently prolific to be grown in broad drifts to create bold horizontal splashes of colour. Many tiny jewels must be excluded, therefore, and enjoyed as pot plants in an alpine house or placed around the edges of a rock garden, where they may be scrutinized at close quarters.

The species are not adapted to the alien conditions of our gardens and if they are to thrive must be given the growing conditions they expect. For most this means fertile, loose,

deep, well-drained soil. The situation should be open and exposed to the uninterrupted sunshine needed to bring them into flower in spring and to bake and ripen their bulbs in summer. In these conditions the bulbs can be left in the ground from year to year, which is a big advantage over many of the garden cultivars.

When content with their situation many species will increase in number. Some will send out droppers, those tough tubular growths that descend deep into the soil to form a new bulb at their tips. Others may spread by stolons and quickly develop into wide patches to appear spontaneously amidst neighbouring plants.

One of the easiest introductions to this group of tulips is *T. tarda*. It is only 4 inches/10 centimetres tall, flowering for many weeks beginning in the middle of the tulip season. The narrow fresh green leaves remain close to the ground, above which rise between two to five flower stems with flowers that open in sunshine to reveal clear yellow petals boldly tipped in pure white. These star-shaped flowers are fragrant and the plants can quickly spread by means of bulbs, stolons and seed to create bold patches of colour around

LEFT AND ABOVE
Tulipa sprengeri

Tulipa bakeri 'Lilac Wonder'

The scented flowers of *T. sylvestris* are bright yellow flushed green and maroon on the outside. Its foliage is long, narrow and vigorous, which can look untidy unless it is grown in the wilder parts of a garden.

The same treatment is also required to persuade *T. bakeri* and *T. saxatilis* to reflower in the relatively dull, moist climate of northern Europe. These species are native to Crete, although populations of *T. saxatilis* have more recently been found in south-west Turkey. They not only benefit from the confinement of any surrounding rocks or tiles: they also gain extra warmth from the stored heat these release throughout cool nights.

The 8 inch/20 centimetre tall triploid *T. saxatilis* is undoubtedly derived from the smaller diploid *T. bakeri*. Its pointed petals are soft lilac with a distinctive yellow base. *T. bakeri* has smaller darker-coloured flowers. Both are distinguished by long, thick, broad and unusual highly glossy leaves. In truth, it is not good taxonomy to treat these as two distinct species and, with *T. saxatilis* being the earlier recorded name, *T. bakeri* should correctly be called *T. saxatilis* Bakeri Group.

T. bakeri is only 4 inches/10 centimetres tall but its cultivar *T.b.* 'Lilac Wonder', taller at 6 inches/15 centimetres, is the one to grow. Its open-faced flowers are light purple, slightly darker on the outside with a dominant large yellow base. These sweetshop colours are not really to my taste, but I cannot see a bed of these happy flowers without admiring their strength of character.

As the tulip season proceeds, *T. acuminata* and the neo-tulipae described on page 70 will come into flower, and may share the stage with a handful of other species which, in my opinion, are amongst the most beautiful tulips worthy of a place in our garden borders. *T. whittallii* is top of my list not least because it is amongst the tallest of these at some 12 inches/30 centimetres when in flower. The bowl-shaped flowers are terracotta orange which darkens to burnt toffee tints as they mature. They are greenish buff on the outside and the base is dark bronze with a lighter rim; sumptuous is the only

the edges of borders. This species is easy to grow and for many years I was amazed to see it reappear in a root-filled pot on my balcony containing a tall and vigorous birch tree.

Adversity typifies the environment in which many of these species have evolved. Some, when given less challenging conditions, will simply grow their leaves and spread vegetatively, foregoing the need to flower and make seed. The worst example of this is *T. sylvestris*, the wood tulip. Its origin is unknown, but it has been associated with cultivated land, in particular vineyards and orchards, since the sixteenth century in Europe, North Africa, Central Asia and Siberia. It thrives in dry stony soils that become baked hard in the summer. In northern Europe, where it is often found growing in grassland, it rarely gets the summer baking it needs. Here it grows well but flowers only occasionally. Interestingly it also responds to disturbance: when, for example, an old churchyard or orchard has been cleared and the soil dug over, the following spring has seen the spontaneous flowering of plants that had earlier gone unnoticed in the grassy sward without flowering. In a garden it can usually be persuaded to flower well if its roots are confined using stones or tiles sunk into the surrounding soil and if situated in a sun-drenched corner.

Tulipa batalinii 'Bright Gem'

Tulipa batalinii 'Bronze Charm'

Tulipa batalinii 'Yellow Jewel'

Tulipa grengiolensis

Tulipa hageri

appropriate adjective. *T. orphanidea* is said by some botanists to be synonymous with *T. whittallii*, but it is paler in colour and grows poorly in comparison. The cultivar *T.o.* 'Flava' is the stronger-growing, yellow-flowered form usually offered for sale, but I find its flowers pale and insignificant and would not waste time growing it. Evidence suggests that *T. whittallii* is really the more vigorous tetraploid form of

T. orphanidea, and if that is correct we should call it *T.o.* 'Whittallii Group'.

T. hageri is closely related to the afore-mentioned species. The perfectly proportioned bowl-shaped flowers have oval-shaped petals pointed at the tip that are deep red inside with green and bronze tinting on the outside. The flower's large base is greenish black with a diffuse yellow border. The form I grow, *T.h.* 'Splendens',

Tulipa linifolia

Tulipa montana

ABOVE *Tulipa saxatilis* and *Narcissus* 'Hawera' BELOW *Tulipa sprengeri*

is multi-flowered with three to five coppery bronze flowers per stem. These pretty tulips are only 8 inches/20 centimetres tall and can be overwhelmed in a garden border. Mine grow isolated in an open area of gravel with a few low-growing alpines for company.

Bolder and more dramatic than any of these, *T. grengiolensis* grows 16 inches/40 centimetres tall. It was discovered in Switzerland in 1946. The goblet-shaped flowers are clear yellow, irregularly margined in warm orange red. This unique tulip is no doubt related to the neo-tulipae of France and Italy and equally worth preserving in our gardens.

The exquisite form or colouration of some tulips such as *T. whittallii* and *T. hageri* suggest to me that they are best used in discrete situations where they can be admired individually. Other tulips with less distinctive characteristics work better as wider groups bringing drifts of colour across the garden floor. *T. batalinii* is best used in this way. Growing only 6 inches/15 centimetres tall, it resembles a miniaturized version of many modern cultivars. The typical lemon-yellow flowers with a brown base open late in the season and last for many weeks. It is generally accepted that this species is the albino version of another sturdy little tulip, *T. linifolia*, which is bright scarlet red. As such these tulips should be named as *T. linifolia* Batalinii Group and undoubtedly it will be under this name that they will begin to appear in bulb catalogues in the future.

Crosses of these two species have resulted in a group of charming cultivars with larger flowers than either of their parents in shades of apricot and amber. My first choice would be *T. batalinii* 'Bright Gem' (*T.l.* (Batalinii Group) 'Bright Gem'), which has sulphur yellow flowers lightly flushed with orange. Others include 'Yellow Jewel', a paler yellow with light pink blush; 'Apricot Jewel', orange red on the outside and golden yellow inside; and 'Bronze Charm', which has light yellow petals delicately feathered bronze. These subtle colourations call for equally subtle planting companions – low-growing ornamental grasses such as pale green *Stipa tenuissima* or any of the blue-leaved fescues. Scattered amongst the emerging vegetation at the edge of woodland they can bring a sparkling touch of excitement and sophistication.

Over a larger area the different cultivars of *T. batalinii* could be mixed to create a subtly varied harmonious association. For more contrast, red-flowered *T. linifolia* could be included or *T. montana* (syn. *T. wilsoniana*), which is a charming little tulip, growing 6 inches/15 centimetres tall, that is easy to please and readily available. The flowers are deep blood red, the petals broad and rounded with a pointed tip and a very small black base.

And finally, there is one more tulip for the wilder areas of our gardens. *T. sprengeri* should be more widely grown, as it is probably the easiest tulip to be grown in average garden conditions. It tolerates some shade, can be naturalized in grass and does not need soil that becomes dry in the summer months. Like the other species tulips, it can be left in the ground and in fact it would be extremely difficult to lift it each year as the bulbs are sent down at the end of droppers to considerable depths.

T. sprengeri is of medium stature and grows stiffly upright with bright green leaves to 16 inches/40 centimetres. The flower petals are long and pointed, scarlet red on the inside and set off with large yellow anthers. The outer three petals are metallic buff suffused with green on the outside, and when its flowers open in sunshine their rich interiors seem to glow from within golden chalices. Very few gardeners grow this glorious species, as it is rarely offered for sale; if it is, the price is exorbitant, because it is one tulip that hardly ever produces the offsets by which all others are propagated and hence does not fit into modern production systems. *T. sprengeri* produces abundant amounts of seed and this is how it must be increased. Fortunately, it can be as little as three years before the first flowers appear, in contrast to other tulips that take five to seven years to grow from seed to flower. Drifts of this tulip naturalized along woodland edges can bring a dazzling end to the tulip season. Buy just one bulb, sow the seed that it forms directly where it can grow undisturbed, and within less than five years you too can have borders full of this beautiful treasure.

Tulipa sylvestris

ABOVE *Tulipa tarda* BELOW *Tulipa whittallii*

COLOUR

We have already seen that the tulip can take many different forms and colours, ranging from the fine simplicity of the Single Early Group to the grotesque of some Parrot Group tulips and the pure white of 'Pax', on to the complexly patterned 'Prinses Irene' and near black of 'Queen of Night'. In the open garden, tulips are grown first and foremost for the colour they bring to a scene, and with the exception of blue and pure black they can easily fulfil this need.

Colours affect our mood and the way we perceive the atmosphere of any place we find ourselves in. This occurs sometimes by association, such as red with heat, yellow with Easter and blue with the sea or cold. Colours may also affect us at a subconscious level; for example, green is said to calm us down, while orange brings excitement and red suggests pleasure and passion.

Spring in my mind is a time for celebration and excitement. My eyes search for the first glimmers of its arrival and once it is in full swing I want to see wide sheets of yellow, green, white and gaudy orange. With the help of tulips and daffodils I can realize my ideal. Such associations and aspirations are at the heart of good garden design as they guide us towards planting schemes that realize and emphasize our passions.

Bulbs are usually the last group of plants to be added to a garden and they lend themselves to being easily squeezed in amongst its existing components. When planted in sufficient quantity tulips can be used to bring bold sweeps of colour to borders and indeed the whole garden. I urge you to widen your horizons and use tulips with confidence, filling your brush and boldly painting your canvas with the same confidence as an expressive artist.

You might maintain colour themes throughout the season, with different groups of tulips succeeding one another, or alternatively you might switch the atmospheres: first bold and vibrant, later cool and sophisticated. With different tulips flowering at different times across a season spanning some ten weeks, there are many possibilities. My front garden is more sober and formal than the rest of the garden and in early spring the colour theme is gentle and harmonious, but just before the tulip season ends a bold splash of vibrant magenta provided by the Single Late tulip 'Grand Style' plays out the final crescendo. The rear garden is different: yellows, oranges and reds are given their head throughout the spring as here the celebration of its arrival is in full swing out of sight of my timid neighbours.

In the sections that follow I have gathered tulips together into colour groups that attempt to reflect their use in planting designs. With tulip colouration being so complex, some flowers could possibly be included in more than one place. I have based my choices on application. I have grouped together white and very pale-tinted flowers, as they are used to lighten a planting scheme, but when their tint is the main reason for growing them I have included them with the yellow, pink or violet groups as appropriate. Likewise, the violet and purple section deals with a wide range of differently coloured flowers which share the fact that they display clear-coloured tones that make definite contrasts with reds, oranges and yellows.

By using the index you can find fuller descriptions and illustrations of many of the tulips in the previous section, Twenty Classic Tulips.

ORANGE, TOFFEE AND TERRACOTTA

The names of these colours are enough to get our taste buds twitching and trigger a host of other warm associations. These are the colours of spices, Seville oranges and Mediterranean rooftops. They represent joy and excitement, in tones that are deep and reassuring – unlike yellows, which can be bright, light and frivolous.

Orange is a bold, dominant colour that can never be expected to nestle in the background. It shouts for attention, but in nature the pigments that create it are complex, producing colour effects that, although persistent, are rarely tiring and overpowering, as can be the case with excesses of scarlet and sunshine yellows. Conservatively we should contain such a powerful colour, placing it in discrete groupings in parts of the garden that are discovered during a tour rather than across the lawn in full view of everyone, but in spring I feel we should throw caution to the wind. Confidence in design is everything. Splashes of orange here and there will quickly create a bitty effect, but fill the canvas as far and as wide as you are able and the effect can be sensational: not dabs of orange then, but torrents like rivers of molten lava.

The first orange tulip to flower is the short-growing multi-flowered *T. praestans*. The most frequently encountered is 'Fusilier', which is best described as carrot orange, the same flower colour as the equally popular variegated-leaf form 'Unicum'. I would like to use it more extensively. The problem is that its stature means that its leaves quickly become submerged by the foliage of other perennials and it fails to reappear in subsequent years, which is why I confine it to the edges of paths. Towards the end of its flowering it overlaps with the start of the Fosteriana season and the first blooms of the exceptional tulip cultivar 'Cantata'. Its flowers are the identical shade of orange as *T.p.* 'Fusilier', but the petals are adorned by a metallic bronze outer flame. Its shiny bright green leaves – it is one of the few tulips to have these – are far more attractive than the typical glaucous green of most garden hybrids.

Challenging *T. praestans* for the 'first orange tulip to flower' spot is the Kaufmanniana 'Early Harvest'. The flower colour is far deeper and more complex; the underlying base colour is rich yellow, which is to be seen clearly around the petal edges, overlaid with dark vermilion red to create the overall orange effect. Such rich colouring calls for darker-toned companions, as might be provided by the fissured texture of brown bark or mounds of the bronze form of the evergreen sedge *Carex comans*.

Since orange is formed by combining red with yellow, there are a couple of Fosteriana tulips that appear orange from a distance. The most strident of these is 'Juan', worth growing as much for its heavily marked foliage as its large elongated orange red flowers with a clear yellow base that is visible from the outside when the flowers are closed and even more so when they are held wide open in sunshine. 'Toulon' is similar but slightly shorter at some 16 inches/ 40 centimetres tall.

My preferred choice out of the Fosteriana assortment is 'Orange Emperor'. The flowers are much smaller, and their colour of clear orange is made lighter by the glow from its pale buttercup yellow base. The petals have a paler-toned outer flame which is streaked and flushed green especially when the flowers first open. Although orange, this tulip does not scream it at you and is easily mixed with other coloured flowers without overpowering them. 'Orange Emperor' in particular is very persistent in the garden; planted slightly deeper than normal it will reappear year after year. The glamorous, very similar 'Orange Brilliant' is well worth growing, but its more intense colour is far less easily placed.

Orange is a prevalent colour of Greigii Group tulips. Some are pure orange, albeit in a medley of tones, as in 'Orange Elite' and 'Orange Toronto', while many more are orange created by overlaying patterns of red, yellow, peach and salmon tints, as in 'Cape Cod', 'Compostella' and 'Oriental Splendour'. For garden borders these tulips seem too artificial to associate with other spring perennials and are best used in pots. The exception is my favourite, 'Easter Surprise', which has relatively small flowers, light orange at their tips fading to clear glowing yellow at their bases.

Single Early tulips, slightly preceding the Greigii tulips in the sequence of flowering, and seem to offer the best and the worst of what orange can mean. 'Generaal de Wet' is the most sublime toffee orange tulip we can have in our gardens, but 'Flair' with its buttercup yellow flowers splashed and streaked with vermilion is vividly shocking. 'Apricot Beauty' is really too delicate a shade to be considered here, but its sport 'Bestseller' is more richly coloured and maybe just sneaks in; the colour is a complex mixture of coppery orange and pink.

There are some gardeners who declare orange to be a vulgar colour that should be avoided but at the same time consider the Triumph 'Prinses Irene' to be the ultimate in sophistication. Such inconsistencies are the spice of life and 'Prinses Irene' can justify being the exception that proves their rule. The perfectly shaped flowers are a dark shade of orange heavily streaked with purple that effectively modulates their impact.

If orange needs to reach a climax, it should surely be in the mid season with the flowering of the Darwinhybrids. These huge, bold, sturdy tulips come in many shades of red, yellow and orange, and when in flower dominate everything both far and wide. Many of the hybrids have flowers in which red and yellow mix to create orange, as in 'Apeldoorn Elite' and 'Banja Luka', but perhaps one of the purest orange tulips of any is the first Dawinhybrid introduced, 'Oranjezon'. Its sport 'Lighting Sun' is decidedly more vivid, with a pink flame on the outside petals that fades to a light yellow around their edges.

I find 'Ad Rem', a typical bold variety with scented orange scarlet flowers edged with yellow, and 'World's Favourite', similar but even richer in colour, too heavy in the garden when compared to the lighter tones of one of my 'classic' tulips, 'Daydream'.

Considering the number of Triumph tulips there are, it is surprising how few are orange. There is 'Orange Monarch', deep orange suffused with tones of pink and amber; 'Cassini', a brownish red that in strong light looks orange; and its sport 'Orange Cassini', in which this effect is far more pronounced. The brightest of all is 'Prins Claus', a sport of 'Judith Leyster'. The flowers are a flamed yellow over tomato red to create glowing orange bowl-shaped blooms.

I am always excited when I encounter 'Montevideo' as it seems to capture all the exuberance of the Darwinhybrids but in a considerably more compact form that is more in scale with private gardens, as is also the case with 'Prins Claus'. The pale yellow rounded flowers, heavily feathered with orange and rose, seem to glow like lanterns even on the sunniest of days. And finally the best orange Triumph tulip of all must be 'Annie Schilder', named after a famous Dutch singer of the 1960s. The colour is a rich brown and orange overlaid with hues of pink and yellow, far more beautiful than words can describe.

Equally fine, though unfortunately, nowadays, rarely offered for sale, is the Single Late tulip 'Dillenburg'. Each flower is a medley of orange and terracotta with the bonus of a sweet scent.

The lower-growing multi-flowered tulips have their uses at the front of borders. 'Orange Bouquet' is one of the best and its colour is deep and saturated. Lighter in its impact, but still intense, especially with back lighting, 'Colour Spectacle' — bearing numerous canary yellow flowers which are heavily streaked and feathered with shades of dark red — is one of the very last tulip hybrids to flower.

There are of course orange double tulips and the most famous of these is 'Oranje Nassau', an early-flowering variety. For a late display the choice must go to 'Orange Princess', the double sport of 'Prinses Irene', which bears the same sophisticated colour palette within beautiful sturdy petal-filled blooms.

For variety one could grow the deep-toned Fringed tulip 'Noranda', the Darwinhybrid sport 'Fringed Solstice' which is guaranteed to make your friends reach for their sunglasses, or the demure, low-growing 'Fringed Beauty'. Parrot tulips can also add to the mix and might include pale 'Apricot Parrot', deeper 'Orange Favourite' and glowing 'Monarch Parrot'.

Within the Lily-flowered Group there are some delectable orange toffee concoctions to play with. First on my list will always be 'Ballerina', with its rich-toned, perfectly formed and intensely fragrant blooms. 'Aladdin' is more spidery, with flowers that are in truth scarlet edged with yellow but come across as a russet. With its dark brown red petals broadly edged with orange, 'Queen of Sheba' is the most exotic of all. And finally 'Jane Packer', which is more red than orange, but emanates the same intense vitality of all the other members of this challenging colour group.

Orange tulips will harmonize readily with reds and yellows and make vibrant contrasts with blues and purples; they will be enriched when surrounded by darker tones, but they can overwhelm soft pale tints. To use them in a small garden will present many challenges but may bring fabulous rewards. And don't forget that if they turn out to be too much you can always pick them and use them as cut flowers.

Key

Group

D	Darwinhybrid	SL	Single Late Group
DE	Double Early Group	T	Triumph Group
DL	Double Late Group	V	Viridiflora Group
Fo	Fosteriana Group		
Fr	Fringed Group		
G	Greigii Group		
K	Kaufmanniana Group		
L	Lily-flowered Group		
M	Miscellaneous		
P	Parrot Group		
SE	Single Early Group		

Flowering time

early season ●————————

mid season ————●————

late season ————————●

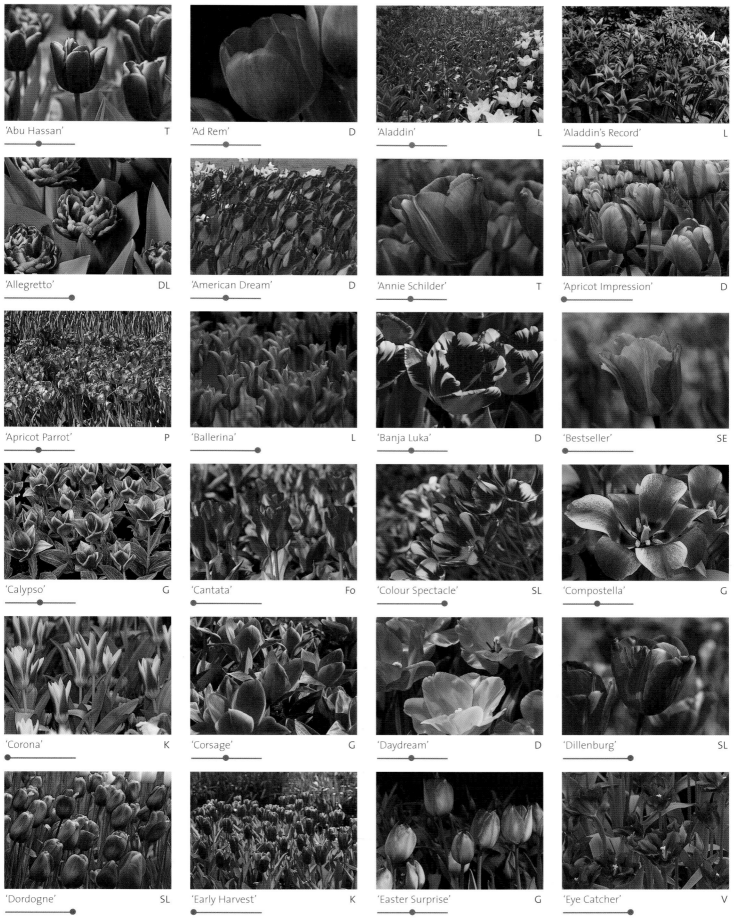

'Abu Hassan'   T

'Ad Rem'   D

'Aladdin'   L

'Aladdin's Record'   L

'Allegretto'   DL

'American Dream'   D

'Annie Schilder'   T

'Apricot Impression'   D

'Apricot Parrot'   P

'Ballerina'   L

'Banja Luka'   D

'Bestseller'   SE

'Calypso'   G

'Cantata'   Fo

'Colour Spectacle'   SL

'Compostella'   G

'Corona'   K

'Corsage'   G

'Daydream'   D

'Dillenburg'   SL

'Dordogne'   SL

'Early Harvest'   K

'Easter Surprise'   G

'Eye Catcher'   V

'Flaming Parrot'   P

'Flowerdale'   G

'Fringed Beauty'   Fr

'Fringed Solstice'   Fr

'Gavota' & 'Warsowa'   T

'Generaal de Wet'   SE

'Georgette'   SL

'Gudoshnik'   D

'Jane Packer'   L

'Juan'   Fo

'Lambada'   Fr

'Lighting Sun'   D

'Love Song'   K

'Margot Fonteyn'   T

'Mary Housley'   T

'Monarch Parrot'   P

'Montevideo'   T

'Nizza'   DL

'Noranda'   Fr

'Orange Bouquet'   T

'Orange Brilliant'   Fo

'Orange Cassini'   T   'Orange Emperor'   Fo   'Orange Monarch'   T   'Orange Princess'   DL

'Orange Queen'   D   'Orange Toronto'   G   'Oranje Nassau'   DE   'Oranjezon'   D

'Princess Margaret Rose'   SL   'Prins Claus'   T   'Prinses Irene'   T   'Professor Röntgen'   P

'Quebec'   G   'Queen Ingrid'   G   'Queen of Sheba'   L   'Temple of Beauty'   SL

Tulipa acuminata   M   *Tulipa grengiolensis*   M   *Tulipa hageri*   M   *Tulipa praestens* 'Fusilier'   M

Tulipa praestens x *albertii*   M   *Tulipa schrenkii*   M   *Tulipa whittallii*   M   'World's Favourite'   D

YELLOW

As the colour of daffodils and newly hatched chickens, yellow is to my mind the colour of spring. It is also a positive, warm and welcoming colour, and it is to be found in the petal colour of tulips of all classes. Sitting near the centre of the visible spectrum, it is the most intense and saturated colour of all. In one direction, it can pass through citron and chartreuse, becoming green and then cool blue in the other, ochre to orange and on to the warmth of red. In these and all its tints and shades, it is a colour that can exhibit many characters, from fresh and clean to warm and mellow.

Since yellow sits so near to green, yellow-flowered tulips harmonize with the green foliage that surrounds them. Problems some people have with yellow later in the year arise when its intensity dominates other colours in the garden, especially in late summer and autumn, but in spring, things are different: yellow and other primary colours are dominant, and so is bright green. Pink in all its tints is overwhelmed in the summer garden by yellow; just think of pink roses with heleniums and sunflowers. In spring, however, the same pinks when present are never timid but rather produced in vast mounds of colour atop trees and bushes of almond and cherry which easily compete with the drifts of yellow at their feet.

A yellow theme is established in most gardens during spring when primulas, daffodils and forsythia come into flower. Yellow tulips can be grown alongside to reinforce the theme and maybe to extend its duration. Tulips alone could of course be used to establish the same theme, but by mixing plants of different forms and characters the garden is generally more interesting and most likely less formal. As ever, we must make a choice.

With so many yellow tulips to choose from, their flowering times, heights and colour differences will again need to guide our choices. For an early splash of yellow nothing can beat 'Corona', the Kaufmanniana hybrid with huge wide-open flowers and a fire red disc at their centre for added drama. Pure rich yellow 'Berlioz' or 'Franz Léhar' in white with a bold yellow centre are equally spectacular. All these look fantastic in pots.

In my own garden, I grow the Kaufmanniana tulip 'Stresa' to kickstart the tulip season. It is not the first tulip in the garden to flower, but it is the first that I use in sufficient numbers to have a dominating impact. 'Stresa' has small flowers for its class and these are less likely to be damaged by wind and rain. They are clear yellow boldly splashed with red and always in flower before the end of March. A flower like this in July would be considered vulgar, but in spring it brings a lively youthful spirit to the garden. A few weeks later the Single Early tulip 'Prins Carnaval' could take over the same colour palette if you liked.

Double-flowered tulips such as 'Monsella' in bright yellow with fine, irregular, orange red-streaked petals and the deeper pure yellow 'Monte Carlo' have given me great pleasure as pot plants. However, in the garden, I prefer single-flowered tulips, and for the early to mid season the Fosterianas are among my favourites. Just a few 'Yellow Purissima' or the slightly darker 'Golden Purissima', standing 22 inches/55 centimetres tall, with large urn-shaped flowers will have a dramatic impact upon their surroundings.

I have heard people remark that the Lily-flowered tulip 'West Point' is a harsh, even a vulgar shade of yellow. All I can say is that the ones that appear randomly through my patio border, amidst a mass of 'Spring Green' tulips, bring a crucial sparkle to the planting scheme. The flowers open wide in sunshine, resembling spiders hanging at the end of gossamer threads. Given this characteristic, probably the biggest mistake to make with 'West Point' is to plant the bulbs too close together, and undoubtedly this is where the negative comments arise. The recently introduced 'Yellow Spring Green' could replace it in my garden border if I chose, but the colour is more lemon yellow and the effect would then be different.

Darwinhybrids offer many well-known yellow varieties to use in appropriate situations. In contrast, there are surprisingly few yellow Triumph Group tulips to choose from for the mid season. Every bulb catalogue offers 'Golden Melody' and it is well worth growing; however 'Makassar' in dark canary yellow and 'Fortissimo' in a paler buttercup yellow would be my first choices if I could find a supplier. Pure yellow 'Strong Gold' and 'Yellow Flight' are both good alternatives. While production of these two is increasing, 'Makassar' in comparison is rapidly disappearing.

I particularly chose the large-flowered late-flowering tulip 'Big Smile' for a bed in the garden filled with the ornamental grass *Calamagrostis* x *acutiflora* 'Overdam' (see page 59). The light yellow flowers harmonize with the fine yellow/white variegation on the grass's leaves, and at over 24 inches/60 centimetres tall its flowers are held clear of their quickly growing neighbour. Its parent 'Mrs John T. Scheepers' is comparable in scale, with its huge flowers being a deeper shade of yellow.

Yellow when combined with white becomes less strident. By mixing yellow and white tulips together you can develop delightfully fresh schemes. Other plants that can provide a white accompaniment are shrubs such as *Ribes sanguineum* 'White Icicle', brooms and azaleas; perennials such as *Pachyphragma macrophyllum* and *Brunnera macrophylla* 'Betty Bowring'; biennials including *Lunaria annua* var. *albiflora*, *Hesperis matronalis* and *Myosotis sylvatica*; not to mention innumerable other spring-flowering bulbs.

Blue contrasts with yellow, as will drifts of low-growing *Scilla siberica*, *Chionodoxa forbesii* and *Muscari armeniacum* with early- and mid-season-flowering tulips. Later, ceanothus may be used to colour the background, while earlier the hanging bell-like flowers of *Clematis alpina* can serve the same purpose, scrambling over a low support.

Foliage contrast can also play an important role. Yellow- or cream-variegated shrubs such as *Elaeagnus* x *ebbingei* 'Limelight', the holly *Ilex aquifolium* 'Myrtifolia Aurea Maculata' and *Euonymus fortunei* make good backgrounds, as do some of the golden-leaved conifers and dark-leaved berberis. Perennials with bronze foliage, including *Heuchera micrantha* var. *diversifolia* 'Palace Purple' and *Ligularia dentata* 'Desdemona', can be dramatic. Don't forget also yellow-variegated *Symphytum* 'Goldsmith' and hostas later in the season.

Good companions might also include crown imperials (*Fritillaria imperialis*), euphorbias and wallflowers in shades from pale yellow through to deep maroons, and also cold-season ornamental grasses such as *Carex elata* 'Aurea', luzulas and the calamagrostis mentioned earlier. Small yellow-flowered shrubs that are complemented by yellow tulips in early spring include *Kerria japonica*, *Coronilla valentina* subsp. *glauca* 'Citrina' and *Edgeworthia chrysantha*.

'Berlioz'   K

'Big Smile'   SL

'Candela'   Fo

'Corona'   K

'Dancing Show'   V

'Elegant Lady'   L

'Fidelio'   T

'Fortissimo'   T

'Franz Léhar'   K

'Giuseppe Verdi'   K

'Glück'   K

'Golden Apeldoorn'   D

'Golden Artist'   V

'Golden Harvest'   SL

'Golden Melody'   T

'Golden Present'   T

'Golden Purissima'   Fo

'Goudstuk'   K

'Hamilton'   Fr

'Helmar'   T

'Hocus Pocus'   SL

'Jan van Nes'   T

'Johann Strauss'   K

'Keizerskroon'   SE

'Makassar'   T

'Mickey Mouse'   SE

'Mona Lisa'   L

'Monsella'   DE

'Monte Carlo'   DE

'Mrs John T. Scheepers'   SL

'Prins Carnaval'   SE

'Sapporo'   L

'Stresa'   K

'Sweetheart'   Fo

Tulipa batalinii 'Bronze Charm'   M

Tulipa batalinii 'Bright Gem'   M

Tulipa batalinii 'Yellow Jewel'   M

Tulipa tarda   M

'West Point'   L

'Vlammenspel'   SL

'Yellow Purissima'   Fo

'Yellow Spring Green'   V

'Yokohama'   T

RED

Hot and horny, red is the colour to get our adrenalin pumping. This is the colour of stop lights, emergency buttons and human blood. Outside in a garden it will attract attention, and when brightly lit, foreshorten distances; conversely, on a dull day it will probably disappear. This comes about as a result of red's position at the very edge of the colour spectrum, its long wavelengths drifting off into invisible infrared, which we can only register as heat. As a consequence red is best appreciated at close quarters in the garden, where we can fully indulge in its richness.

The year when I planted 'Red Shine' – the tall, late Lily-flowered tulip – into a border of ornamental grasses and effected a spectacular transformation was when my love affair with tulips began. As green registers directly opposite red on the colour wheel as its complementary colour, a green setting for red makes a strong contrast. Grasses seem an appropriate choice, even a lawn, but a bed filled with freshly emerging shuttlecock ferns (*Matteuccia struthiopteris*) and tall red tulips came over to me as disturbing since I know the fern comes from a damp woodland setting and the tulip from open, sun-baked slopes. Daylilies produce fresh sheaths of foliage very early in the year and these I would find easier to assimilate, but most perennials are showing their new foliage by early May and can provide the necessary background for red tulips.

Should you visit the Keukenhof garden in the Netherlands when it opens in late March, early spring, you will find that the park is predominantly green with a calm that precedes the explosion of colour that will soon follow. At this time, one red tulip is repeated around nearly every turn to sensational effect. This is the Kaufmanniana hybrid 'Showwinner'. This waterlily tulip is clearly indispensable as, together with the equally early-flowering 'Stresa' in yellow and red, it is capable of making a convincing show for the first of the visitors. Flowering so early, however, Kaufmanniana tulips all run the risk of being damaged by bad weather, and all too often I have seen the Keukenhof display browned and shrivelled by hard frosts and drying winds. 'Showwinner' reacts by losing its radiant glow and its colour darkens, and it is worth looking at only as a splash of colour in the distance. In our smaller gardens, we can still exploit the early season of 'Showwinner' by growing it in pots and giving it protection when the weather turns nasty.

The next spectacular red to flower is the well-known Fosteriana tulip 'Madame Lefeber', which is sometimes erroneously called 'Red Emperor'. Its large fiery red flowers open to reveal a bold black base edged in yellow. The colour of this species was unrivalled when the first bulbs were imported into Holland in 1906, and ever since it has been used in breeding programmes with great success. As the stems are not really strong enough for the heavy flowers, to avoid disaster in rain and wind grow her in a sheltered corner, with maybe an evergreen background for a truly spectacular display, albeit ephemeral and quite likely short lived.

Red-flowered Greigii Group tulips offer the bonus of broad purple-streaked leaves. 'Red Riding Hood' is a favourite with many gardeners and 'Margaret Herbst' is taller with extremely large bold flowers. Grow these in pots, leaving the space in your borders free for bold displays of the later-flowering varieties.

The only red tulip you are likely to be offered from the Single Early Group will be 'Merry Christmas', its cherry red colour falling outside my idea of a real red tulip. When the new sports of 'Flair' become more widely available this situation will change, as 'Red Paradise' and 'Red Revival' are both true to their names.

By mid season, the choice of red-flowered cultivars explodes with the commencement of flowering of the Darwinhybrids. As a group, their colour range is predominantly red, orange and yellow. 'Red Impression' will be in flower before most others in the group. It is an imposing blood red tulip growing 22 inches/55 centimetres or more tall. Probably the most famous tulip of all, and the one planted repeatedly on traffic islands and in public parks the world over, is 'Apeldoorn', with its huge scarlet flower with a yellow outer base and the base inside pure black edged with yellow. 'Oxford', with a clean yellow base, and 'Parade' are two more red Darwinhybrids. Of the three, 'Oxford' produces the largest replacement bulbs with fewer offsets in the garden and therefore reliably returns to flower in subsequent years without being lifted. An attempt to reproduce the cross that created 'Apeldoorn' resulted in 'Lefeber's Memory', which is yet another excellent dark red.

Although most red tulips in the Triumph Group have been selected for their suitability for forcing as cut flowers and are not always good in the garden, 'Charles' is good on both counts and has persistently returned to flower in my garden for many years without lifting. It produces a fine

scarlet red flower with a yellow base in mid-April. An equally good choice would be another Triumph called 'Hollandia' which is darker, a rich blood red colour.

The colour of 'Couleur Cardinal' is unique, being scarlet red on the inside, and its outer flame of plum purple give the flowers an iridescence as if it were connected to the electricity supply. 'Rococo', its Parrot sport, is equally exciting with exotic smouldering red flowers.

In comparison 'Bastogne', at over 24 inches/ 60 centimetres, is one of the tallest in this group. Its dark blood red flowers never fail to stop me in my tracks when I come across them; again it is a dark sultry colour that glows with an unrivalled richness when lit from behind. Some other more conventional red Triumphs for the garden are 'Ben van Zanten', 'Capri', 'Friso', 'Hollandia' and 'Sevilla'.

By early May the garden is at its most dynamic, with everything growing quickly in the warmer temperatures and freely available moisture. With so much lush greenery, red late-flowering tulips are an obvious choice where dramatic contrasts are needed. The Single Late Group offers some excellent choices as these tulips are tall and able to keep their flowers above any nearby burgeoning perennials. It includes 'Kingsblood', in exactly the same colour as my favourite 'Red Shine'. 'Halcro' has a pinkness to its red flowers that might almost exclude it from this section, but in the case of 'Cashmir' there is no such doubt. Here the flowers are a bright red with a yellow base. Lower-growing 'Red Georgette' is useful late in the season for bedding as it is a multi-flowered tulip with up to six small flowers per stem. This tulip has its counterpart in the Triumph Group in 'Roulette', which flowers much earlier, around the middle of April.

If Fringed Group tulips appeal, as well as the sport of 'Couleur Cardinal' called 'Arma', there are two others of use to gardeners: 'Hellas' and the award-winning 'Red Wing'.

Species tulips contain some spectacular red-flowered forms. Two that I have grown for some years are *T. montana* (syn. *T. wilsoniana*), a low-growing plant that thrives in scree conditions at the side of one of my garden's gravel paths, and *T. sprengeri* (see page 143).

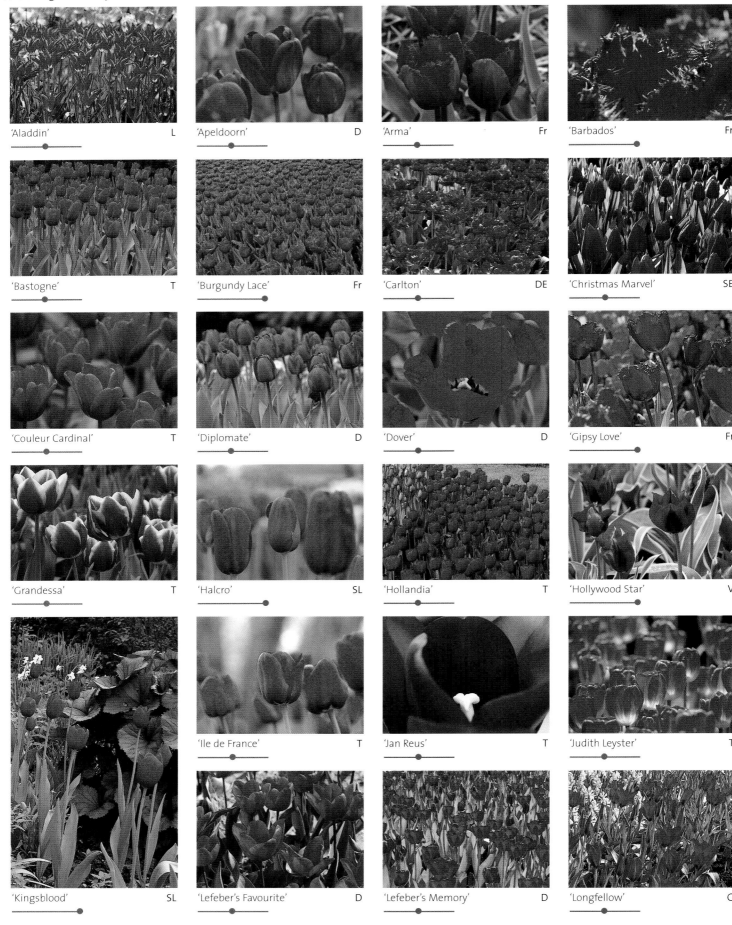

'Aladdin'   L

'Apeldoorn'   D

'Arma'   Fr

'Barbados'   Fr

'Bastogne'   T

'Burgundy Lace'   Fr

'Carlton'   DE

'Christmas Marvel'   SE

'Couleur Cardinal'   T

'Diplomate'   D

'Dover'   D

'Gipsy Love'   Fr

'Grandessa'   T

'Halcro'   SL

'Hollandia'   T

'Hollywood Star'   V

'Ile de France'   T

'Jan Reus'   T

'Judith Leyster'   T

'Kingsblood'   SL

'Lefeber's Favourite'   D

'Lefeber's Memory'   D

'Longfellow'   G

'Plaisir' G

'Madame Lefeber' Fo

'Oscar' T

'Pretty Woman' L

'Red Impression' D

'Red Riding Hood' G

'Red Shine' L

'Robassa' Fo

'Rococo' P

'Roulette' T

'Sevilla' T

'Showwinner' K

'Solva' Fo

Tulipa eicheri 'Clare Benedict' M

Tulipa linifolia M

Tulipa montana M

Tulipa planifolia M

Tulipa praestans 'Red Sun' M

Tulipa praestans 'Unicum' M

Tulipa sprengeri M

'Uncle Tom' DL

VIOLET AND PURPLE

Violet is clear and vibrant, a true spectral colour; purple, in contrast, is dark and complex, made up from a mixture of blue, violet and red. Together these colours sit on the cooler side of the colour wheel and make contrasts with their opposites, the warmer reds, oranges and yellows. However with purple, the opposing character of these two groups of colours overlaps, allowing sumptuous harmonies between shades of bluish red and dark reddish purple. Numerous terms exist to describe the group of colours dealt with here, such as violet, lilac, lavender, mauve, purple and plum, with modifiers such as light, dark, intense and rich, and very few of these will mean exactly the same thing to everyone. Their intensity will also vary with the type of light they are experienced in, which, as we have already seen, can have a very big effect on the way we perceive the pigments in the petals of tulip flowers.

True blue tulips do not exist, even though some bulb catalogues may try to convince you otherwise. The nearest we can come is with the Single Late Group tulip 'Bleu Aimable', its sport 'Blue Parrot' and possibly the Double Late tulip 'Blue Diamond'. In strong light these can all be seen to contain red pigments and consequently appear to be different shades of violet and mauve, but in soft light and dull conditions their blueness is enhanced.

The group of tulips I describe here may all be used for their clear tonal qualities, which will create subtle harmonies when they are mixed together or definite contrasts when associated with hotter colours from the red, orange and yellow part of the spectrum. Purple is the darkest of them all, but rather in the bright glowing form expressed in the Triumph tulip 'Negrita' and not in the near black tones of Triumph 'Paul Scherer', plum purple 'Black Parrot' or dark maroon 'Queen of Night'.

Weeks before any tulips begin to flower, *Crocus tommasinianus* decorates the edges of the paths in my garden with its slim-stemmed violet goblets. I grow the rich-coloured form 'Ruby Giant' for its greater impact. No sooner than it begins to fade, *Tulipa humilis* 'Violacea Black Base' begins to open its rather similar-shaped flowers. The colour is lighter and pinker, but just as impressive. This little species is available in a range of forms and tints, all of which are valuable for bringing contrast to the blue scillas and pulmonarias that dominate the garden this early in the season.

There is a surprising dearth of these colours throughout the early part of the tulip season and the only Single Early tulip is a variety from 1860 called 'Van der Neer'. The colour is a good strong violet purple, but rarely is it offered for sale. It is not until the arrival of the Triumphs in the mid season, starting around the middle of April here in the Netherlands, that these colours appear in any quantity.

Although all other colours are to be found in the assortment of Triumph tulips, it is the large number of violet and purple cultivars that sets them apart. 'Negrita' is the classic purple here, being vigorous, easy and coloured in a tone of purple that glows with the intensity of a stained glass window. Others already described include 'Attila' and 'Passionale', both violet purple; 'Barcelona', light purple; violet pink 'Don Quichotte'; comparatively low-growing 'Purple Prince', with mid-purple flowers; and 'Hans Anrud', deep purple with distinctive black stems.

The Single Late Group contains some of the most desirable cultivars in this colour range, which are worth growing in their own right rather than as secondary additions to a scheme simply to meet the need for some colour contrast. The most delicate tone is to be found in 'Bleu Aimable'. Although it grows 24 inches/60 centimetres tall its flowers are not huge, they are somewhat rounded and bob around in an informal manner. 'Cum Laude' has a larger flower in a slightly darker shade of violet, but like 'Bleu Aimable' it can at times look almost blue. 'Greuze' is a much brighter-glowing purple, but in a significantly darker tone than that seen earlier in the flowers of 'Negrita'. The darkest of all is 'Recreado', a deep violet purple with fairly small flowers held only 20 inches/50 centimetres tall. The interior of its flowers together with their black base intensifies its depth of colour and the contrast it can bring against paler-coloured companions. 'Atlantis' has two-tone flowers, amethyst violet with a broad white edge. Regrettably, the older varieties in the Single Late Group such as 'Bleu Aimable', 'Cum Laude' and 'Greuze' are rapidly disappearing from commercial production.

Lily-flowered tulips always attract attention and when, as in the case of 'Burgundy', they are dark and richly coloured they can find a place in many different planting schemes. 'Burgundy' is deep pure purple and said to grow 20 inches/50 centimetres tall, but with me it is always taller. There are a number of other Lily-flowered cultivars in hues that would readily harmonize with each other: vibrant violet purple 'Lilac Time'; 'Maytime', a darker reddish violet with a narrow creamy white margin to its petals; and 'Ballade', magenta purple with petals edged with a bold white margin.

As I have already said, I am not too keen on double tulips, but there are two late-flowering cultivars that are extremely useful for complementing other taller-growing tulips and for their colour: 'Blue Diamond' and the similarly coloured 'Lilac Perfection', soft lilac fading to white towards the centre of its flowers.

One of the species tulips began this look at violet and purple forms and another is waiting to round it off, the late-flowering *Tulipa backeri* 'Lilac Wonder'. This is probably the easiest of the various forms of this species to grow in the open garden. The light purple flower petals are a slightly darker shade on the outside, with a large yellow base on the inside, which is prominently displayed when the flowers are facing the sunshine.

The violet and purple tulips have a sophisticated air that is lacking in the brasher yellows, reds and oranges. The fact that they predominate in the mid and later part of the season is useful as they can be used in so many subtle combinations where pinks and violets occur as, for example, with the pink blossom of cherry trees and the dangling lockets of bleeding hearts (*Dicentra spectabilis*). In years when their seasons overlap, the violet tassels of wisterias or the billowing masses of blue ceanothus can further make dramatic backgrounds. For contrast use yellow, as might be provided by Bowles's golden grass (*Milium effusum* 'Aureum') or his sedge *Carex elata* 'Aurea', and for real excitement think about orange or the less strident terracotta of *Euphorbia griffithii* 'Dixter'.

'Adriaan T. Dominique'   V

'Arabian Mystery'   T

'Atlantis'   SL

'Attila'   T

'Ballade'   L

'Barcelona'   T

'Baronesse'   SL

'Black Beauty'   SL

'Black Hero'   DL

'Black Parrot'   P

'Bleu Aimable'   SL

'Blue Champion'   T

'Blue Diamond'   DL

'Blue Heron'   Fr

'Blue Parrot'   SL

'Blue Pearl'   SL

'Burgundy'   L

'Cum Laude'   SL

'Don Quichotte'   T

'Gander'   T

'Greuze'   SL

'Hans Anrud'   T

'Lilac Perfection'   DL

'Maytime' L

'Muriel' P

'Paul Scherer' T

'Negrita' T

'Passionale' T

'Pentagon' SL

'Purple Prince' SE

'Queen of Night' SL

'Recreado' SL

'Reliance' SL

'Shirley' T

'Synaeda Blue' T

Tulipa bakeri 'Lilac Wonder' M

Tulipa humilis 'Persian Pearl' M

T.h. Violacea Group black base M

T.h. Violacea Group yellow base M

'Violet Bird' V

'Van der Neer' SE

PINK

When red is diluted with white it becomes pink, but while red means fire and drama, pink is pleasant and welcoming, a colour with its own distinct character. It ranges from the palest tints that function like white to brighten and lift a composition to shocking pink and magenta which are charged with blue and thrust themselves forwards for our attention. These stronger shades are notoriously difficult to use in the garden and some gardeners avoid them at all costs, but without them pink could easily become insipid. Tulips cover this range in its entirety from the palest tint of 'Pink Jewel' to the pure pink of 'Queen of Bartigons' and the vibrancy of 'Blenda'.

In the earliest part of the season true pink tulips are scarce. The Kaufmannianas contain a number of bicoloured flowers that look pink from a distance such as 'Heart's Delight' and 'Ancilla', whose creamy-coloured flowers become pink as they age. The Greigii tulips likewise have pink-hued cultivars such as 'Queen Ingrid' and 'Czaar Peter' which are, in reality, dark pink edged with cream. 'Dreamboat' and 'Rockery Master' might also qualify in the same way along with the Fosteriana tulip 'Dance'.

However, within the Botanical tulip groups there are a number of cultivars with salmon pink flowers that are very definitely not red such as the Kaufmanniana 'Shakespeare', the Fosteriana 'Spring Pearl', and the Greigiis 'Sweet Lady', 'Perlina' and the popular multi-flowered 'Toronto'.

Truly pink tulips exist in the Single Early Group. 'Christmas Dream' is rich pink fading to a paler tone around the edges of its petals; 'Christmas Marvel' is a darker pink. 'Merry Christmas', cherry red to crimson, probably falls outside of the term pink but makes a very good contrast with the others. The sport of 'Apricot Beauty' called 'Beauty Queen' is a beautiful blend of pinks and salmon, but it is not a very sturdy garden tulip. The Double Early 'Peach Blossom' and the much darker 'Queen of Marvel' are both excellent in pots.

You will find many shades of pink Triumph tulips offered by different bulb firms. The pink purple 'Barcelona' is possibly the darkest shade we might include in this selection. More typical clearer pinks are the delicate and silky 'Peerless Pink' and the brighter tinted 'Rosario'. 'Meissner Porzellan' has white flowers that are prominently edged and streaked with shades of warm pink and 'Peer Gynt' and 'Leo Visser' are much stronger tints to experiment with. 'Blenda' is an even more intense dark rose hue with a prominent white base; its flowers seem to radiate energy when lit from behind. 'Page Polka' is similar and could be substituted for it. There is also 'New Design', which has variegated margins to its broad leaves and a pale yellow flower fading to light pink towards the petal edges, and 'Garden Party', whose crisp white flowers boldly edged in carmine red have a bold pink effect. 'Dynasty' is a strong pink with a white base that is rapidly gaining popularity; it is similar to 'Rosario' and the Single Late 'Dreamland' which it is destined to replace.

Where big bold pink tulips are needed, which is unlikely to be the case in my own garden, you could use Darwinhybrids such as candyfloss pink 'Pink Impression', soft pink 'Salmon Impression, shocking pink 'Van Eijk', white and rose red 'Tender Beauty' or the more subtle 'Ollioules', pale pink fading into pure white towards the edges of its petals. Personally, I would substitute any of these with the tall-growing deep pink Lily-flowered tulip 'Jacqueline'. Also, 'Jan van Zanten's Memory', with two-tone pink petals that pale towards their edges, is striking; and for something shorter 'China Pink' is a good strong pink with a white base and a faint bronze blush on the outside of its petals.

Towards the end of the tulip season, pink tulips are extremely good in association with the many woody plants that come into flower in our gardens at this time. Those with unusual flower shapes are always appealing, and as well as the many fine Lily-flowered pinks there are a number of good Fringed cultivars to think about. 'Fancy Frills', 18 inches/45 centimetres tall with delicate white flamed pink petals, is one of the prettiest, as is 'Huis ten Bosch', less red and more mauve. 'Pink Wizard', almost white with a gentle tracery of pink, is an ideal tulip for mixing with other stronger tones.

Pink is found in many of the complex flowers in the Viridiflora Group. 'China Town' is outstanding, with soft pink petals fading towards their edges with bold light green flames and variegated leaves. 'Groenland' is much taller, 22 inches/55 centimetres, with pale white green petals edged in light pink, the same colours as its dramatic Parrot Group sport 'Green Wave'.

The Single Late Group has many different types of pink tulip numbered in its ranks – for example, 'Dreamland', a strong red pink with a bold, contrasting ivory outer flame. For evenly coloured mid-pink flowers we can choose between 'Clara Butt' and 'Queen of Bartigons' or the slate pink crumpled blooms of 'Picture', and when a really tall tulip is needed 'Menton' can be used.

Additionally, there are a number of white- and red-streaked cultivars that give the impression of pink, such as Lily-flowered 'Marilyn', Double Late 'Carnaval de Nice', and Single Late 'Cordell Hull' and its sports, and 'Sorbet'.

To end with, we must not forget the most feminine of all tulips, the soft, apple blossom pink flowers of Double Late 'Angélique', a sight to melt the hardest heart.

'Angélique'   DL

'Beau Monde'   T

'Beauty Queen'   SE

'Blenda'   T

'Carnaval de Nice'   DL

'China Town'   V

'Christmas Dream'   SE

'Dance'   Fo

'Doll's Minuet'   V

'Douglas Bader'   SL

'Dreamboat'   G

'Fritz Kreisler'   K

'Grand Style'   SL

'Gander'   T

'Garden Party'   T

'Green Wave'   P

'Groenland'   V

'Heart's Delight'   K

'Huis ten Bosch'   Fr

'Jacqueline'   L

'Jan van Zanten's Memory'   L

'Lydia'   T

'Make-up'   T

'Mariette'   L

'Marilyn'   L

'Meissner Porzellan'   T

'Menton'   SL

'Murillo'   DE

'New Design'   T

'Ollioules'   D

'Page Polka'   T

'Peach Blossom'   DE

'Picture'   SL

'Pink Diamond'   SL

'Pink Impression'   D

'Pink Jewel'   SL

'Pink Wizard'   Fr

'Queen Ingrid'   G

'Queen of Bartigons'   SL

'Renown'   SL

'Rosario'   T

'Toronto'   G

'Sorbet'   SL

WHITE AND LIGHTER SHADES OF PALE

Pure light is white, brighter and more persistent than any other colour. In truth, in nature it is rarely pure but rather created by pigments that introduce slight casts of other colours such as pink, violet, blue and yellow. Surface textures also alter the way a colour appears, and in the case of tulip petals their silk-like qualities make them shine brilliantly.

White is an important colour in the garden. Other colours when placed near it seem to gain in intensity and brightness, while colour clashes can be eliminated by using white flowers as a buffer. Their prominence makes them effective in introducing formality through repetition to a planting scheme or garden space. Bold clumps of white tulips framing an entrance or on the corners of flower borders reinforce the architecture and ground plan of the space, but they can also be used in quantity, creating wider drifts of lightness which make everything seem more open and wider apart.

When you are adding tulips to planting associations to bring accent and to focus attention, white tulips are as effective with other white and pale-tinted companions as they are in darker, contrasting colour schemes. Against dark green backgrounds, typically formed by yew and box hedges in gardens, they stand out dramatically, their elegant upright form giving them added impact.

Since white will turn a pure tone into a pastel tint, white tulips can be used in mixtures with other tulips to lighten their impact and create gentle blends that harmonize more easily with their surroundings. Tulips with slight colour casts are especially useful in this way when the colour cast can be linked with the same stronger hue exhibited by companions in the mix.

I have extended the scope of this section to go beyond white to other pale-tinted tulips which, although clearly pale shades of pink, violet or yellow, are primarily of use as light elements in planting designs. Since the line drawn between these and the cultivars I have placed in the other colour sections may at times be questionable, when you need a pale-coloured tulip of a particular shade it would be advisable to look not only here but in the appropriate colour section as well.

Some of the earliest white tulips to flower are *Tulipa biflora, T. turkestanica* and *T. polychroma.* Although pretty, with small flowers and yellow bases, these are all species for the rock garden or pot and not important plants for creating bold effects in the open garden. The first group of tulips we might consider using in this respect are the waterlily tulips, the Kaufmannianas, but none of these is truly white. Some, however, are very pale-tinted such as the type species

(*T. kaufmanniana*) and 'The First', which is a very pale yellow with faint red markings. Even lighter 'Franz Léhar', with its bold, purple-flecked foliage, and 'Ancilla', which becomes pinker with age, are probably the best candidates for adding lightness in the back of a shrub border.

As for the other Botanical tulips, there are no white Greigii tulips, nor really any white Fosterianas. Even though one of the best, 'Purissima', carries the nickname 'White Emperor', this magnificent tulip has a yellow base and is far from pure white – to me it is creamy yellow. For an earlier true white, we need to look into the Single Early Group, where there are a couple of possibilities. 'Diana' is an excellent pure white, typical in every way. In comparison, 'White Christmas' might be considered more interesting. Its distinctly pointed white petals have a greenish tinge with a pale primrose yellow outer flame, making it ideal for blending with yellow-flowered tulips or other perennials.

If early double flowers are called for, you could try the old 'Murillo' sport 'Schoonoord', which is often available, but 'Cardinal Mindszenty' is preferable as it has better form and robustness. In the Double Late Group 'Mount Tacoma' is the only real choice and it is one of the few double-flowered tulips I would expressly recommend to other gardeners. Its pure white flowers are beautifully formed and occasionally streaked green on the outside, which only seems to add to its interest. New white hybrids from 'Monte Carlo', such as 'Bel Air', 'Evita' and 'Mondial', promise to be gardenworthy as well when they become generally available.

Of the Triumph tulips – the maincrop tulips, so to speak – 'Pax' is my standard white. When, as often is the case, it returns to flower without having been lifted, it flowers even earlier, so using it effectively does away with the need to think about using Single Early tulips in my borders. The flowers are a pure untainted white, almost glassy in appearance. 'White Dream' is the most frequently offered white Triumph and a good garden variety, even though you need to lift the bulbs for summer storage. I have yet to grow the new 'Calgary'. The plants have a solid, formal appearance and seem ideal for introducing

formality and repetition along the front or at the corners of borders, and with its long flowering period, easily a month, its future looks promising.

If only one white tulip were allowed, the choice would have to fall on the Lily-flowered Group's 'White Triumphator'. The flowers are large but avoid being gross by way of their elegant pointed petals. During flowering, they keep growing, as all tulips do, and often become very tall, but even when they are knocked to the ground by storms, they rise again like serpents to regain their refined poise.

The Fringed tulip 'Swan Wings' should never be forgotten; this is another robust garden performer in the purest of whites available. The fine-fringed petals add interest to the blooms. Where interest needs to be replaced by intrigue, there is the large-flowered 'White Parrot' waiting to accept the role.

With creamy yellow petals with the characteristic green stripes on their outsides standing out boldly, less strident than pure white, the Viridiflora 'Spring Green' is a tulip to lighten almost any planting scheme.

'Maureen' is unquestionably the classic white tulip to end the season. Its large flowers confirm the fact that it is one of the many offspring of the robust Single Late tulip 'Mrs John T. Scheepers'. At 27 inches/70 centimetres tall, it is one of the tallest tulips grown, which is of course a useful characteristic this late in the season.

The palest of pink tulips to use as white in coordinated schemes include Triumph 'Beau Monde', Fringed 'Pink Wizard', Viridiflora 'Groenland' and Single Late 'Pink Jewel'. And some of the palest yellows in the assortment are Lily-flowered 'Sapporo', which fades to white as it ages, and Single Late 'City of Vancouver', quite often the very last tulip hybrid to be seen flowering in the Keukenhof garden each year.

Finally, some of the white tulips that bear light traces of colour around the edges of their flowers, which may or may not increase and develop in intensity as the flowers age, can also be used to add light to planting associations. These include the Triumphs 'Mata Hari', 'Skagit Valley' and 'Shirley', and the Single Lates 'Grand Slam', 'Magier' and 'Montgomery'.

'Beau Monde'   T

'Calgary'   T

'Casablanca'   DL

'City of Vancouver'   SL

'Concerto'   Fo

'Franz Léhar'   K

'Green Eyes'   V

'Johann Strauss'   K

'Maureen'   SL

'Magier'   SL

'Mount Tacoma'   DL

'Pax'   T

'Skagit Valley'   T

'Purissima'   Fo

'Sapporo'   L

'Shirley'   T

'Spring Green'   V

'Swan Wings'   Fr

'Très Chic'   L

Tulipa clusiana   M

Tulipa polychroma   M

Tulipa turkestanica   M

'White Triumphator'   L

'White Dream' with 'Lilac Perfection' and 'Picture' (Triumph/Double Late/Single Late)   T

COLOUR MIXTURES

Take a bag of red tulips and another of white, mix them and you will have a mixture that six months later will have flowered and look pink from a distance. Nothing could be easier, and with so many coloured tulips to play with the possibilities are endless. Yet it is surprising how rarely this is done.

Some tulips do the job for us, flowering with two or more colours adorning their petals. Care is needed in mixing these with others, as it can quickly lead to chaos. What does work well is mixing a two-tone tulip, such as yellow and red 'Prins Carnaval', with another tulip that picks up one of these colours, such as cherry red 'Merry Christmas'. For these mix effects to work we need to choose tulips that flower around the same time. In this example, the tulips are both from the same group, the Single Early Group, and therefore have similar flowering times. Another way to guarantee this is to mix together cultivars with the sports they have generated. The Double Early tulip 'Murillo' is probably the best example, having produced more than a hundred sports over the years in diverse colours, all of which flower at more or less the same time.

Colour blends that mix tulips to flower at the same time can be as simple or as complex as seems appropriate. You might mix just two cultivars or, alternatively, two groups of cultivars: one group to supply one tone, say red, and the other group to supply either a contrasting tone, say white, or a harmonious tone, say purple. Colour blends that are more complex might include a wide range of colours that in some way or other combine to give a specific effect. A blend might, for example, bring together a wide range of violet and purple tones. It might go further and include additional mauves and pinks, or have orange added to change the effect from sophistication to the outright fun of the fair.

Simple or single-tone blends are probably the most successful and with care you can carefully control them to change and alter the atmosphere in the garden as one walks from one area to another. With a higher percentage of a lighter tone in one place and a gradual change to a richer tone in another, you can steadily increase the sense of enclosure and drama.

Creating a blended colour in this way, which might be varied in intensity and tone by varying the proportions of the cultivars included in the mix, is one reason for mixing tulips. A second reason is to maintain a colour theme over an extended period by including cultivars that flower in succession. You might, for instance, choose an orange theme for an area of the garden. It could begin with *Tulipa praestans* 'Fusilier'; two weeks later the Fosteriana tulip 'Cantata' could supply the same tone, eventually to be overtaken at the height of spring by massed displays of Darwinhybrids such as 'Oranjezon' and 'Apeldoorn Elite'. The toffee orange Lily-flowered tulip 'Ballerina' might bring in a more sophisticated and darker tone later in the season and in its turn hand over to pure orange 'Dillenburg' for its final contribution to the theme.

In one border of my own garden, I have tended to combine the two approaches to mixing tulips by setting a colour theme and adding different cultivars to keep the theme going throughout the whole of the tulip season. The theme is violet, which extends to mauve and purple with some magenta for highlights. It starts with *T. humilis* Violacea Group black base then Single Early 'Christmas Dream', which is pink, and contrasts with purple 'Van der Neer'. Triumphs dominate the main season, including 'Attila' and 'Passionale', both violet purple, light purple 'Barcelona', violet 'Demeter', and violet pink 'Don Quichotte' and 'Purple Prince'. The Fringed tulip 'Blue Heron' puts in an appearance and the season runs on with the Single Lates: dark violet 'Cum Laude', glowing purple 'Greuze' and deep violet purple 'Recreado'.

Although I have mixed these tulips together randomly, I could have used them in discrete clumps for a more controlled effect. A coordinated scheme spread out along the length of a long border could start with 'Christmas Marvel' and move through 'Barcelona' and 'Purple Prince' to 'Negrita', and as always clumps of white 'Pax' could be interplanted to lighten and extend it.

More formal effects can be achieved when the tulips are not actually mixed but planted in alternating blocks or rows. This approach particularly suits pathways leading to entrances and spaces that are more public. By ordering the patterns, you can place later-flowering cultivars in front of one another to flower progressively and thereby retain the design.

As with colour, flower shape can also be used to bring differentiation to a mixture. A mix of Lily-flowered and conventional single-flowered tulips in harmonizing colours works well; for example, tall, deep rose pink 'Jacqueline' with the lower-growing single Triumph silky pink 'Peerless Pink'. However, too great a contrast can easily become distracting. I have seen the rich purple Lily-flowered tulip 'Burgundy' overpower a mixture with red, orange and amber tulips. Also, colour contrast can become too harsh, as I noted once with a mixture of pure white 'White Dream' and purple 'Negrita' tulips, which from a distance looked fine but near by lacked any refinement.

Many varieties mixed

A commercial blend – 'Gemengde Lexion'

Mixed Lily-flowered tulips

'Queen of Night' and 'Shirley'   T

'Calgary' and 'Seadov'   T

Mixed tulips in grass

Mixed Fosteriana tulips

'Negrita' and 'Shirley'   T

'Banja Luka', 'Gavota' and Kees Nelis'   D, T, T

'Negrita' and 'Yokohama'
                                           T

GROWING TULIPS

Seeds

Seed is probably the least likely method gardeners will use for increasing their stock of tulips, for not only will it take from five to seven years for the first flowers to appear, but the results will be unpredictable and highly variable, since garden tulips are the result of decades of hybridization. Knowing this, we remove the spent flowers in order to redirect the plant's energy into the formation of next year's bulb and any offsets that might form around the base of the mother bulb.

Seed capsules, when allowed to form, will be found to contain hundreds of triangular seeds neatly stacked one above the other. While in the case of the garden hybrids these may be of no use to us, they can offer a means of raising large numbers of species tulips, which not only come true from seed but also start flowering a lot sooner than garden hybrids since their mature bulbs are much smaller. In a rock garden setting where the soil is rarely disturbed, you could simply scatter the seed and allow nature to take its course. Alternatively, seed can be sown in pots. I have been doing this for some time with *Tulipa sprengeri*, which I would like to encourage to grow in wild, naturalized drifts in the wilder areas of my garden, because the bulbs are rarely available and always expensive. I sowed the seeds in wide terracotta pots containing gritty compost. Unlike most seeds, these need to be sown deeply and I covered them with

½ inch/1 centimetre of compost and a thin top layer of gravel. In the first year the growth in the pots resembled grass; by the time this died down in summer, tiny white bulbs had formed. These bulbils should be harvested and stored in sand through the summer and replanted ½–¾ inches/1–2 centimetres deep in September. In my case this didn't happen and the bulbs were simply left in their pots; however, I renewed the top couple of centimetres of compost and applied a light dressing of bonemeal and they reappeared the following year without any sign of distress, and they had significantly broader leaves. Although *Tulipa sprengeri* will come into flower within three years of sowing its seed, in my case I suspect it will take four, but by that time I will have over a hundred bulbs from the first year's sowing and more to follow in each subsequent year. In this case, definitely, the small amount of effort involved will be generously rewarded.

Bulbs

When growing strongly in ideal conditions, the replacement bulb that the tulip produces each year from an internal bud in the mother bulb, and possibly some of the offsets it produces around the base (see page 10), should be big enough to flower the following year, but any that are not can be grown on in a nursery bed for a couple of years until they make larger

LEFT Exhibition display under trees

bulbs. This is the main method used in the commercial production of all garden tulips and we can copy it if need be. In the case of most cultivars the effort is probably not worthwhile as tulips are not expensive; however, rare or historic cultivars that are only occasionally available would certainly justify the time and space they take up.

In the Netherlands, fields of tulips are allowed to come into flower for just as long as it takes for the growers to check that the plants are not infected with tulip breaking virus and that they are true to type. The flowers are then cut off and the bulbs left to grow until their leaves begin to wither and turn yellow. These vast fields have been one of the main sources of new tulip cultivars as tulips display a very high incidence of mutation, resulting in sports that exhibit different colours or flower shapes from their parents. As the growers walk through their fields they remove any diseased or erroneous plants and mark any potential sports for further investigation.

The bulbs are ready for harvesting around the end of June to the middle of July. The soil is shaken from the roots and they are spread out to dry in a cool airy place. As gardeners, we can follow the same system. Different cultivars and species will ripen at slightly different times, but for each the ideal time for harvesting is when the foliage has started to shrivel and before it easily detaches from the new bulb, as at this later stage it becomes more difficult to trace and harvest all the bulbs.

The bulbs are then cleaned or, as they say in Dutch, peeled: the dried-up skins of the mother bulb and the spent flower stalk are pulled away to leave a clean new bulb wrapped in its brown tunic. Although the tunic helps protect the bulb during storage and handling, if it splits and falls away this causes no real problems; however, the bulbs then need to be handled very carefully to avoid bruising.

Store them or leave them in the ground?

Some tulips can and must be left in the ground from one season to the next. To start with, the species tulips are usually left alone. In part this is because they must be provided with improved growing conditions to thrive and this will make their perennialization more likely. As we have seen, in their native habitats tulips grow in soils that are baked hard and dry in the summer, so we need to give them an exposed sunny site that remains open during the summer months with soil that is deep and well drained. Another reason is that many increase by sending out stolons horizontally or droppers vertically, which produce new bulbs at their tips at considerable distances from the mother bulbs. To try to dig up all these is often impossible and the species involved thrive anyway; they situate their bulbs in favourable conditions and not only reappear each year but also usually increase in number. This is the case with the Botanical tulips in particular: the Kaufmanniana, the Fosteriana and the Greigii tulips.

The question always arises, 'What about the other tulips? Can we also leave them in the ground?' The answer is complex, but in principle you will obtain the best results by lifting the bulbs and storing them properly until the autumn, when it's time to return them to the soil. In our garden soils, which are far damper than a tulip's origins would favour, there is really nothing to be gained by leaving them buried during the summer. Firstly, they lie waiting as potential victims for slugs, which have a habit of crawling down the narrow tunnel left when the flower stalk dies and devouring them ravenously. Secondly, the bulbs will flower earlier the following year than those planted late in the autumn. This can cause problems in our northern European climate, where repeated frost and thaws can damage the emerging shoot tips and make them more susceptible to fungal infections.

So as far as the bulk of the garden hybrids are concerned, you should lift them when you can and retain the largest bulbs for the following year's display. However, this is not always easy, especially when the bulbs are being used in borders mixed in amongst other perennials and shrubs. In this case the best advice is to grow those tulips with a reputation for perennializing and to plant them far deeper than normal. Deep planting seems to reduce the number of offset bulbs they produce and hence puts more energy into replacement bulbs. Throughout this book I have attempted to highlight the best bulbs to use in this way as I personally find it impossible to lift my bulbs as a consequence of the way I weave them into border planting schemes. I accept that there will be losses each season and continuously top up the displays each year. In general the garden hybrids most likely to reflower, in addition to the species and Botanical tulips already mentioned, are Darwinhybrids, Lily-flowered tulips, some Fringed tulips and some, but by no means all, Single Late tulips. Many of the very old cultivars still surviving in today's assortment have done so because of their ability to cope with this treatment such as 'Generaal de Wet', 'Couleur Cardinal' and 'Mrs John T. Scheepers'.

Storage through the summer needs to be in a cool, dry and, most importantly, airy place. A garage or attic is ideal so long as it is not hot and stuffy, and mice must be excluded: in such conditions tulip bulbs turn to a jelly-like consistency and die; mice will devour any bulbs to which they can gain access.

Timing of planting

Throughout the summer months tulip bulbs are far from dormant. They are growing slowly and internal changes are occurring that lead to the development of the embryonic flower bud, its stem and leaves. Commercial growers of tulips monitor these changes carefully and give the bulbs a series of hot, warm and cool treatments to trigger the various stages in their development. For the cut flower trade this is essential, as by providing different temperatures for different lengths of time growers can prepare the bulbs to flower at exactly the moment required. The hot treatments are designed to convince the bulbs that they have been through a hot dry Asian summer; the cold treatment is needed to trigger extension growth and flowering. For bulbs that are going to be forced with heat into flowering, the length of stem is very important and it has

been found that the longer the cold treatment the longer these will eventually become. Every cultivar is different, and there are specialized companies in the Netherlands that have the expertise and facilities to bring not only tulips but other bulbous plants as well into flower on any date in the year; this is especially important for exhibition purposes.

As gardeners we too must ensure that our bulbs experience a long cold period before their spring flowering time. In England the traditional date for planting tulips was always said to be on the day of the Lord Mayor's Show, which takes place in the City of London every second Saturday in November. But London is a long way from the north and west of the country and weather conditions vary from year to year, making this date nothing more than a useful indication. Small offset bulbs being grown on to flowering size should be planted in early autumn around September. For the rest, late autumn is ideal as this provides at least six weeks of cool growing conditions before there is any chance of hard ground frost occurring and delaying root and shoot development. In other countries such as North America, local conditions as indicated by hardiness zone maps should be studied and the tulips planted early enough to give this six-week period, during which the plants will begin to send out their roots. And in the southern States where it never freezes, tulip bulbs need a six-to-twelve-week storage period in the salad drawer of the refrigerator prior to planting. For those who wish to grow tulips in such places, local bulb suppliers will offer detailed advice; however, to my mind tulips in the tropics seem out of place.

Site, soil and planting

Tulips are very hardy and need the cold; however, cold and damp conditions will kill them. Low-lying sites in which water accumulates in winter or where air circulation is limited should be avoided. Where there is the choice, the tulips should be grown high up on sloping ground and not in a frost pocket. The other consideration is that they need a site that is not buffeted by strong winds. While many of

Bulb field, Lisse, the
Netherlands

the modern hybrids might be able to cope with wind, there are others that will have their blooms damaged by gusts of wind, driving rain or hail. Sites near hedges and fences are often ideal as these offer wind protection while still allowing good air circulation.

Deeply dug (the traditionalists say 20 inches/50 centimetres), well-draining, friable soil, possibly improved by the addition of grit and garden compost, is the ideal growing medium for tulips. However, it is remarkable just what you can get away with. Newly planted tulip bulbs contain plenty of nourishment to assist them to grow and come into flower, and they will do so even when they are unable to form a good root system. That said, you will obtain the best results when the soil is free draining and fertile, and

certainly when you aim to have tulips for later years they must be grown well.

Feeding is not necessary and excess nitrogen will lead to lanky weak growth. A slow-release fertilizer such as bonemeal and garden compost can be added to the soil during its preparation to improve its fertility and structure; and when bulbs are left to grow in the soil from year to year, a light top dressing of these materials in early spring will be beneficial.

The way you arrange the tulips in your garden will, to some extent, determine the method you adopt in planting them. When planting them in rows, as might be the case in the vegetable garden, it is far easier to dig out the soil to the desired depth along the length of the row, space the bulbs out in the loosened soil along the bottom of the trench and then carefully refill it. The same approach might be adopted in beds and borders where there is room, but often this is impossible. The alternative is to dig individual holes for each bulb using a trowel or a purpose-made bulb planter. On my heavy soil, I prefer to use a trowel as my bulb planter cuts a cylinder of soil, making a smooth-sided hole that is difficult for the roots of the bulbs to escape from. However, planting bulbs individually is hard work and always takes longer than you expect.

Too often tulips are not planted deeply enough. In heavy soils some compromise is permissible, but ideally each bulb should be covered by twice its own height with soil. This means that the hole needs to be three times the height of the bulb or on average some 6 inches/15 centimetres deep. Garden tulips are normally planted 8 inches/20 centimetres apart or more, depending upon the effect required. The smaller-growing species tulips can of course be planted closer together and do not need to be quite so deep in the soil.

I wish we could naturalize modern tulip cultivars in grass in the same way as narcissi and crocus, but it does not work. Following planting, the first year's display will look great as the bulbs have their inbuilt reserves to sustain them, but by the second year few if any will return as the competition from the grass is simply too great for them. Only by replanting every year can this sort of scheme be sustained. Success is more likely with species tulips in conditions they find favourable – *T. springeri* in light woodland where grass grows less vigorously, for instance.

I know of gardens in southern Germany, where summers are long and hot, where tulips have naturalized on sun-drenched slopes of low-nutrient soil on which grass grows far less vigorously, but elsewhere 'topping up' will be necessary to sustain the effect – see page 179.

Tulips in pots

When growing tulips in pots, it is important to avoid peat-based potting composts, which can be too acidic for tulips and also hold on to too much water during their winter outside. You can use a soil-based compost such as John Innes No. 2 or a coir-based compost, but in every case you should add sand or grit to improve drainage. You can cram the bulbs into the containers to the point where they are almost touching, and one trick to know is to turn them so that the flat sides of the bulbs face outwards. This causes the first and largest of the tulip's leaves to grow outwards and over the rim of the pot, resulting in a far tidier display. The containers should offer sufficient depth for the roots to grow into and the bulbs should be just covered by the compost. After watering, place the containers somewhere cool and sheltered, and protected from the attention of mice. I place mine in a shady corner at the base of a hedge; or you could put them in a trench and cover them with soil for the winter, or leave them outside in a garden cloche or unheated greenhouse. At no point should they be allowed to freeze solid as this will kill the bulbs. Once they begin to shoot in the spring they need to be placed in full sunlight. No feeding is necessary as the bulbs bring with them their own food reserves and, as explained earlier, once they have finished flowering you should dispose of the plants as they are unlikely to produce bulbs big enough to flower the following year. The important exceptions to this are some of the small species tulips, which can be successfully grown in pots for many years.

Watering

Once you have planted tulips you should water them thoroughly, and if the autumn is dry you should repeat this at regular intervals. This is necessary as the aim is to encourage them to form a good root system before the onset of winter. This applies equally to bulbs grown in the open garden and those in pots.

Likewise during spring, as the bulbs are shooting skywards, and certainly when they are in flower, they should not go short of soil moisture. I have known springs when three weeks at a time have gone by without any significant rain falling, and without watering the tulips' flowering periods were significantly shortened.

Care and the control of diseases

Good garden hygiene is the key to success with tulips. To start with it is important to purchase the very best-quality bulbs and avoid late-season discount offers, which are more than likely to be smaller and often damaged bulbs. All bulbs exported from the Netherlands are carefully controlled to eliminate diseases and must be size 10 or greater. Size is important for guaranteeing top-quality flowers. Sizing is based on the circumference of the bulb; thus a size 10 bulb is at least 4 inches/10 centimetres in circumference. Sizes 11 and 12 are not uncommon, especially with some of the large-flowered Darwinhybrids and Single Late Group tulips. In my preferred bulb catalogues I see that all their bulbs are size 12+, apart from the smaller-growing species, which understandably range in size from 5+ to 8+. Even when you have purchased the best quality available, it is important to check them for any signs of mould or physical damage as these problems will only invite disease once they are in the ground.

During planting it is important to ensure that the bulbs are not bruised or damaged. At this stage one of the biggest problems your bulbs are likely to face are mice as well as other gnawers such as rats, squirrels, moles and voles; and in America I think we could add chipmunks and raccoons to the list. With me, it is field mice; they seem able to smell the bulbs underneath the loose earth. It is said that deeper planting can help reduce the incidence of attack. Be careful to gather up any tunics that fall from the bulbs as you plant them as these will act as signposts for the mice. There is not a lot you can do against these animals; some years my whole garden escapes their attention and others not. It is always the newly planted areas that they dig into. One measure that seems to work is to cover the disturbed soil with a thick layer of gravel. The theory suggests that this falls into the holes the mice make and impedes their progress; for expensive species tulips it is probably worth the investment. Other soil predators include slugs, wireworm and nematodes. You can control these with chemical drenches, but in well-prepared soils they are rarely a major problem.

The most serious disease you are likely to encounter is tulip fire or botrytis, a disease caused by the fungus *Botrytis tulipae*. Every effort will have been made to ensure that this is not present in the bulbs you purchase, but once they are growing in the garden they can become infected. Any damage to the surface of the plants is a potential point of entry for the fungus; infection often follows periods of frost and hail, and it will spread extremely quickly when conditions are damp and rainy. The leaf tips of infected plants become yellow and shrivel, and their shoots may be twisted and the leaves misshapen and streaked with red. Round to oval spots appear on the leaves, first yellow then grey brown with wet edges, at which stage they are termed lesions. In wet weather, whole flowers and stems become covered in mould and eventually dark pinhead-shaped resting bodies form called sclerotia. These can fall and remain viable in the soil for a number of years; spores can be blown on the wind or splashed in raindrops to infect nearby plants. Needless to say all this spells disaster and must be avoided at all costs.

Best practice suggests that you should not plant tulips in the same place for at least three years, but in a small garden that is not always possible. In commercial practice the use of systemic fungicides can virtually eliminate tulip fire, and a spray regime, starting in late winter when the first shoots appear above the ground, at five- to ten-day intervals (depending upon whether the weather is wet or dry), is ideal. However, there are no systemic fungicides authorized for use by gardeners – at least in Europe at present. In truth, I have never felt the need for these as vigilance can work perfectly well if you spot infected plants early, and remove and burn them.

Other fungal diseases can infect tulips ,including *Botrytis parasitica* and grey bulb rot (*Rhizoctonia tuliparum*). Infected bulbs will either fail to grow or appear with stunted or shrivelled shoots and leaves. In every case the methods of control outlined above for tulip fire will be

Bulb field, Lisse, the Netherlands

effective, the golden rule being: if you see an infected plant, dig it out and burn it.

As with most diseases, if the plants are grown well they will be less susceptible. To summarize, purchase top-quality bulbs free from surface damage, grow them in friable soil that has not been excessively fertilized, do not overwater and if possible replant in a different site each year. It is also important to remove any fallen petals and dead flowers immediately, as these can harbour disease. These as well as the dead leaves and flower stems gathered at the end of the season should be thrown away and never added to your compost heap.

The likelihood of diseases occurring increases when bulbs are left in the ground from one year to the next. As well as being at risk from slugs, unlifted bulbs will often appear above the ground before any newly planted bulbs and are,

consequently, more likely to be injured by early frosts and hail. Also, inevitably, some bulbs will become infected by the tulip breaking virus, which is transferred between plants by sap-sucking aphids. This can be controlled to some extent by regular systemic insecticide sprays but is most effectively dealt with by removing plants the moment you see that the flowers are broken and burning them. Vigilance and decisive action are the keys to controlling diseases of tulips in our gardens, just as we see commercial growers scouring their photogenic bulb fields. The infection causes the plain petal colouration to break up into concentrated lines and streaks with paler areas between which, it has to be said, can be quite attractive. The same virus infects lilies, which may also harbour it without showing symptoms. For these reasons tulips should never be planted near lilies.

Index

Page numbers referring to illustrations are in **bold** type
Tulip cultivars are listed alphabetically by cultivar name

Select Bibliography

Baker, Christopher, with text by Willem Lemmers and Emma Sweeney, *Tulipa: a Photographer's Botanical*, Artisan, New York, 1999

This large-format volume is a photographic survey of currently available species and cultivars. The text by Willem Lemmers is fascinating, with a great deal of information about the origins and inter-relationships of various cultivars. The book includes an eloquent essay on the tulip by Michael Pollan.

Classified List and International Register of Tulip Names, Royal General Bulb Growers' Association (KAVB), Hillegom, 1996

This is the bible of cultivar names and tulip classification. Each entry, of which there are over 2,600, includes the name of the grower and the date of registration, if known, together with a precise description of the flower form, colour, height and chromosome count when possible.

Hall, Sir A. Daniel, *The Book of the Tulip*, Martin Hopkinson, London, 1929

This is the classic book on tulips that every enthusiast should read. Written after the identification of tulip breaking virus, it marks a watershed in the history of the tulip. It covers with utter clarity everything from morphology, taxonomy, history and classification to cultivation in the garden, forcing in the greenhouse, seed raising and breeding.

Hall, Sir A. Daniel, *The Genus Tulipa*, The Royal Horticultural Society, London, 1940

This is an academic text on the classification of tulip species, a subject that is still unresolved today. Detailed descriptions of individual species include comments on their suitability for use in gardens.
The text is generously illustrated throughout with drawings and photographs and the final third of the volume presents a series of forty beautiful colour illustrations by H.C. Osterstock.

Jacob, Revd Joseph, *Tulips*, Present-Day Gardening series, J.C. & C. Jaek, London & Edinburgh, 1912

This is my favourite book on tulips, written by someone who knew and loved these plants intimately. Most of the cultivars named are no longer in the assortment, but the ideas on how to use tulips in gardens are still very relevant. Every aspect of their cultivation is described, discussed and eloquently presented.

Pavord, Anna, *The Tulip*, Bloomsbury, London, 1999

This thick book is a *tour de force* covering the entire history of the tulip in minute detail, beautifully illustrated and printed. The latter part of the book includes good descriptions of species and cultivars suitable for growing in British gardens.

Acknowledgments

Author's acknowledgments

I took the photographs for *Gardening with Tulips* over a period of five years and I am indebted to all those who made this possible by opening their gardens to me. Foremost amongst these are the director and staff of Keukenhof in Lisse in the Netherlands. Without the unlimited access to their display garden my task would have been made much harder. Likewise, the collections of the Dutch bulb auction organizations, the CNB and the Hobaho, were indispensable for research and photography. Kees Breed's personal collection of tulip cultivars enriched my forays into these trial grounds which have many rare, old and historically important cultivars no longer in commercial production. In this respect, the collection of tulips maintained at the Hortus Bulborum in Limmen also served as an important source of information and inspiration.

Taking photographs showing the creative use of tulips in private gardens was an essential part of my task and I am particularly indebted to Loekie Schwartz, Marion van Heuven, Evert Warffemius and Frans Koekkoek in the Netherlands and Manfred Lucenz and Klaus Bender in Germany. Christine Orel's planting schemes for the Landesgartenschau in Kaiserslautern and the naturalistic tulip schemes of Cassian Schmidt at the Sichtungsgarten, Hermannshof, in Weinheim were truly inspirational.

Many other gardeners have shared their passion and experience of tulips with me. To all of them, thank you. In particular the day I spent with Carla Teune at the Hortus Botanicus in Leiden gave me a thorough grounding in both their history and husbandry.

Frans Roozen at the IBC (Internationaal Bloembollen Centrum) provided invaluable advice and introduced me to growers and breeders in the commercial sector. Johan van Scheepen assisted my research in the library of the KAVB (Koninklijke Algemeene Vereeniging voor Bloembollencultuur) as well as patiently answering my many questions about the classification and naming of the tulips I had photographed.

Eric Breed's technical review of my text and photographs was essential in guaranteeing that only the best and currently available cultivars and species are included in these pages. His endorsement along with the advice from the IBC and KAVB was both reassuring and invaluable in ensuring the accuracy of my efforts.

In my own garden I have been encouraged and assisted as always by my partner Ton Weesepoel. His help in selecting the photographs and his advice with the layout and design of the book have revealed hidden talents which I hope to be able to take advantage of in the future.

To all who have helped me and share my passion for tulips, a very big thank you.

Photographic acknowledgments

With the exception of those listed below, all the photographs in this book are copyright © Michael King. The publishers have made every effort to contact holders of copyright works. Any copyright holders we have been unable to reach are invited to contact the publishers so that full acknowledgment may be given in subsequent editions.

Private Collection: 17
Teylers Museum, Haarlem, the Netherlands: 21
University Library, Erlangen: 19